D1797102

SexPerfect

THE ART OF SEXUAL INTERCOURSE

Dedication
To the Campbells – may they keep on coming

Drawings by Lynn Paula Russell
Diagrams by Vania Zouravliov

THE *Erotic* Print Society
London 2003

THE *Erotic* Print Society
EPS, 1 Maddox Street
LONDON W1S 2PZ

Tel (UK only): 0871 7110 134
Fax: +44 (0)20 7437 3528
Email: eros@eps.org
Web: www.eroticprints.org

© 2003 MacHo Ltd, London UK
© 2003 Text Dr David Delvin

ISBN : 1-898998-76-0

Printed and bound in Spain by Bookprint, S.L., Barcelona

No part of this publication may be reproduced by any means without the express written permission of the Publishers. The moral right of the author of the text and both artists has been asserted.

THE ART OF LOVE

Sex Perfect

THE ART OF SEXUAL INTERCOURSE

dr david delvin

THE *Erotic* Print Society

Contents

Amor vincit omnia – et nos cedamus amori.

– *Virgil*

Prologue

This is a book for both men and women.

It's all about the nicest activity in the world: sexual intercourse.

You almost certainly know an awful lot about it already. But this volume will help you and your partner to enjoy it a great deal more. And I hope you'll enjoy it safely – and comfortably.

Yes – *comfort* is tremendously important during intercourse.

But quite a lot of people do have problems with discomfort during sex, and that's particularly true of women. (Most men have heard a partner say 'Ow!' loudly in bed…)

Here are a few quick tips for making 'fucking' more comfortable:

- Beforehand, take plenty of *time*. Romance and foreplay help the woman's vagina open up, and her juices flow – so that everything is much more comfortable.
- Consider using lots of *lubricant*. You see, vast numbers of women – and some men – do need some artificial lubrication in order to make things nice and slippery and comfortable. 'Lubes' are often a great help for women who are either under 20 (and possibly

inexperienced) or over 45 (when vaginal dryness tends to start occurring).

•   In fact, it's a great idea to keep a store of agreeable lubricants to hand. Many sexy and sophisticated women over 45 (or post-menopausal women) often have half-a-dozen pleasantly-scented lotions, potions and unguents on the bedside-table so as to be ready for action.

•   These days, you can buy lubricants with no embarrassment at all. Every chemist in Britain sells K-Y Jelly by the ton! But much more erotic liquids and gels are available from sex shops and mail order companies. Good ones include Eros Pjur and Wet.

So before actually beginning intercourse, either of you can 'slurp' lots of lube over the girl's vulva (*see fig 1*). This is in itself a very warm, sensuous activity…

WHAT ABOUT SAFETY?

It's also vitally important to have *safe* sexual intercourse. Unfortunately, the early 21st century has turned out to be a time when all sorts of nasty 'bugs' – from herpes to the potentially lethal hepatitis and HIV – are rampaging throughout the world. Great care is needed in choosing a partner! And if in doubt, always use a condom (male OR female), because it does give a lot of protection.

Obviously, the other great safety risk of sexual intercourse is unwanted pregnancy.

When you're enjoying the glorious delights of fucking, it's all too easy to convince yourself that 'it won't happen.' But as a doctor, I can assure you that it happens all too frequently – particularly when the woman is young and bursting with fertility.

fig 1

So that's another good reason for using condoms. OK, they're not everybody's cup of tea. However, they can actually be *fun* – especially if you make a point of using them as part of your pre-intercourse love-play. The trick here is to agree that it'll be the woman – rather than the man – who puts them on the penis; this is quite exciting for most men.

From the illustration (*fig 2*) you can see how a skilled woman's hands can really arouse a guy's penis as she rolls the sheath onto it!

An alternative technique was apparently developed by Dutch 'ladies of the night' (*fig 3*), where the woman holds the rolled-up condom rather lasciviously between her lips – then she bends her head forward and puts her mouth over her lover's cock. With a little practice, she can easily become adept at unrolling the sheath onto

fig 2
(a) – (b)

his shaft with her tongue. Having this done to you is a delicious experience indeed.

For completeness, a brief word about the *female* condom. You'll see that it's just a simple tube (*fig 4*). A man can gently slip it up into his wife's or lover's vagina – stimulating her with his fingertips as he does so (*fig 5*).

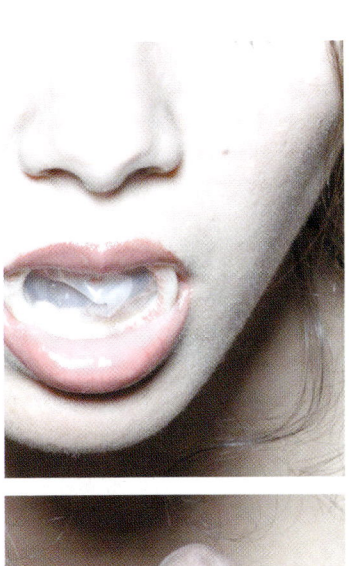

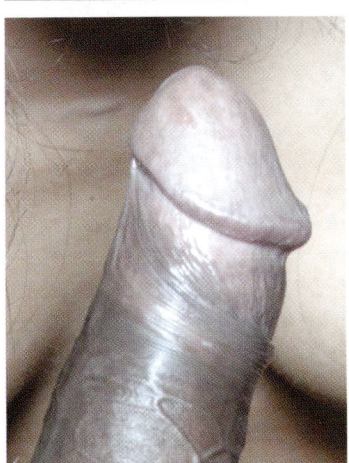

fig 3
(a) – (c)

Experienced men will know that these days, many women protect themselves from pregnancy with the IUD ('coil') or the IUS ('Mirena'). So if you're playing around together before

fig 4

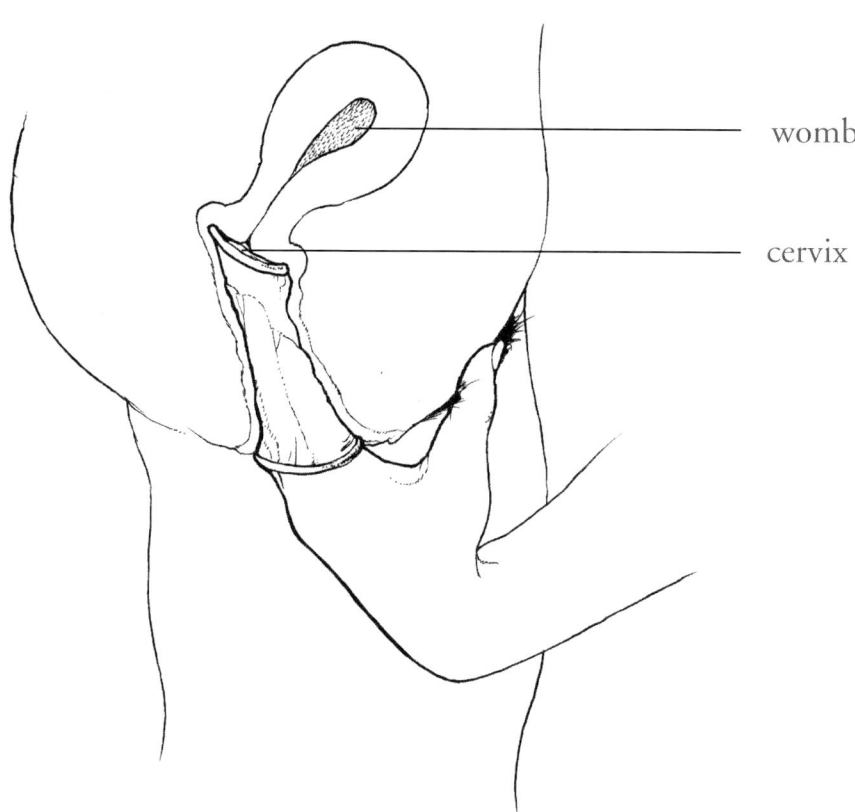

womb

cervix

fig 5

intercourse – with your finger inside her vagina – and you find (*fig 6*) that there is a fine thread hanging down, don't be concerned. It's just a sign that you've picked a partner who knows how to look after herself!

fig 6

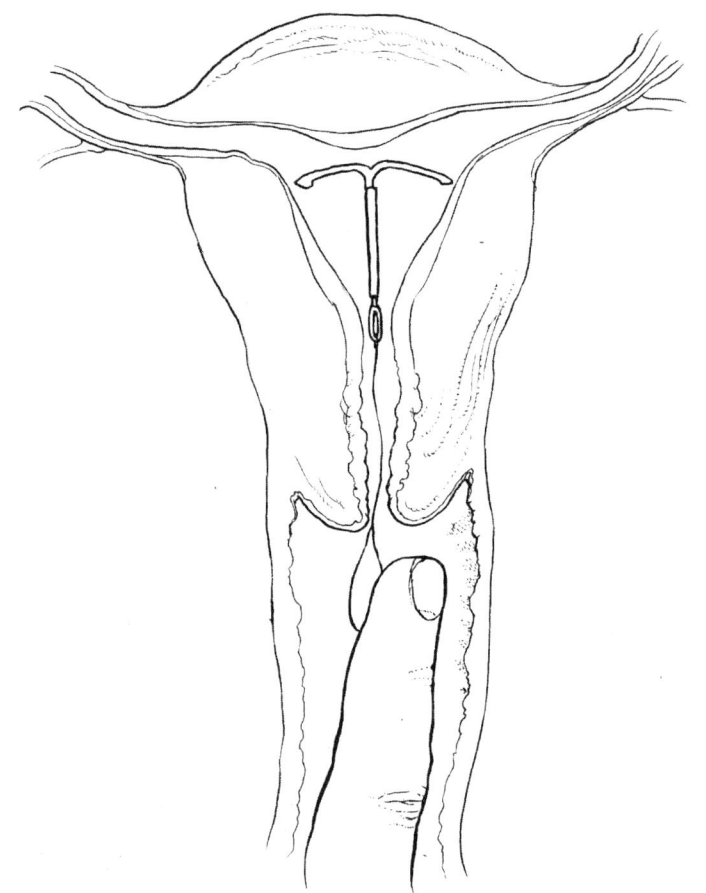

There are many other good forms of contraception, so that these days it should be possible for a man and a woman to have great sexual intercourse together, with practically *no* risk of an 'accidental' baby.

Anyway, I hope that you'll have a lot of fun with this book. Please remember that intercourse is *supposed* to be great *fun*! If the two of you can laugh a lot while you do it, you won't go far wrong.

Don't forget the wise old English proverb:

A maid who laughs is already half-taken...

what happens during intercourse?

So intercourse is the blissful union of the vagina and the penis – at least, I *hope* it's blissful for you!

But let's begin by reminding ourselves of the vital fact that vaginas and penises are made in many shapes and sizes. Fortunately, no matter which way Nature has created them, they're nearly always capable of successful intercourse.

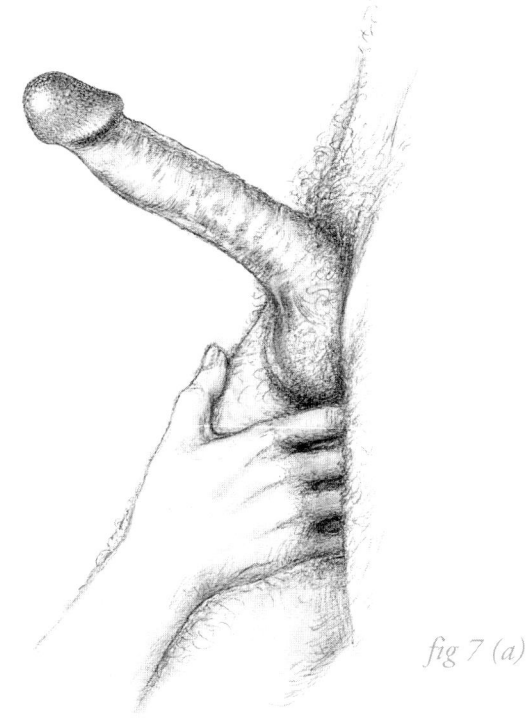

fig 7 (a)

Many men and women don't realise this and think that their sex organs aren't quite 'right' for sexual congress. In particular, men tend to believe that their penises are too small, and women frequently fear that their labia (vaginal lips) are 'too long', or 'too untidy'. I've dealt with hundreds of patients who have been distressed by such fears.

Yet, generally speaking, this distress is quite unnecessary. Almost any penis can satisfy almost any vagina – and vice versa.

If you're a bit worried about your size or shape, do have a look at the illustrations which show a range of penises and vulvas (*fig 7,8*). (The vulva is, of course, the actual opening of the vagina.) Although they vary a lot, they're all normal.

As you can see, some cocks are long, some are short, some are

fig 7
(b) – (d)

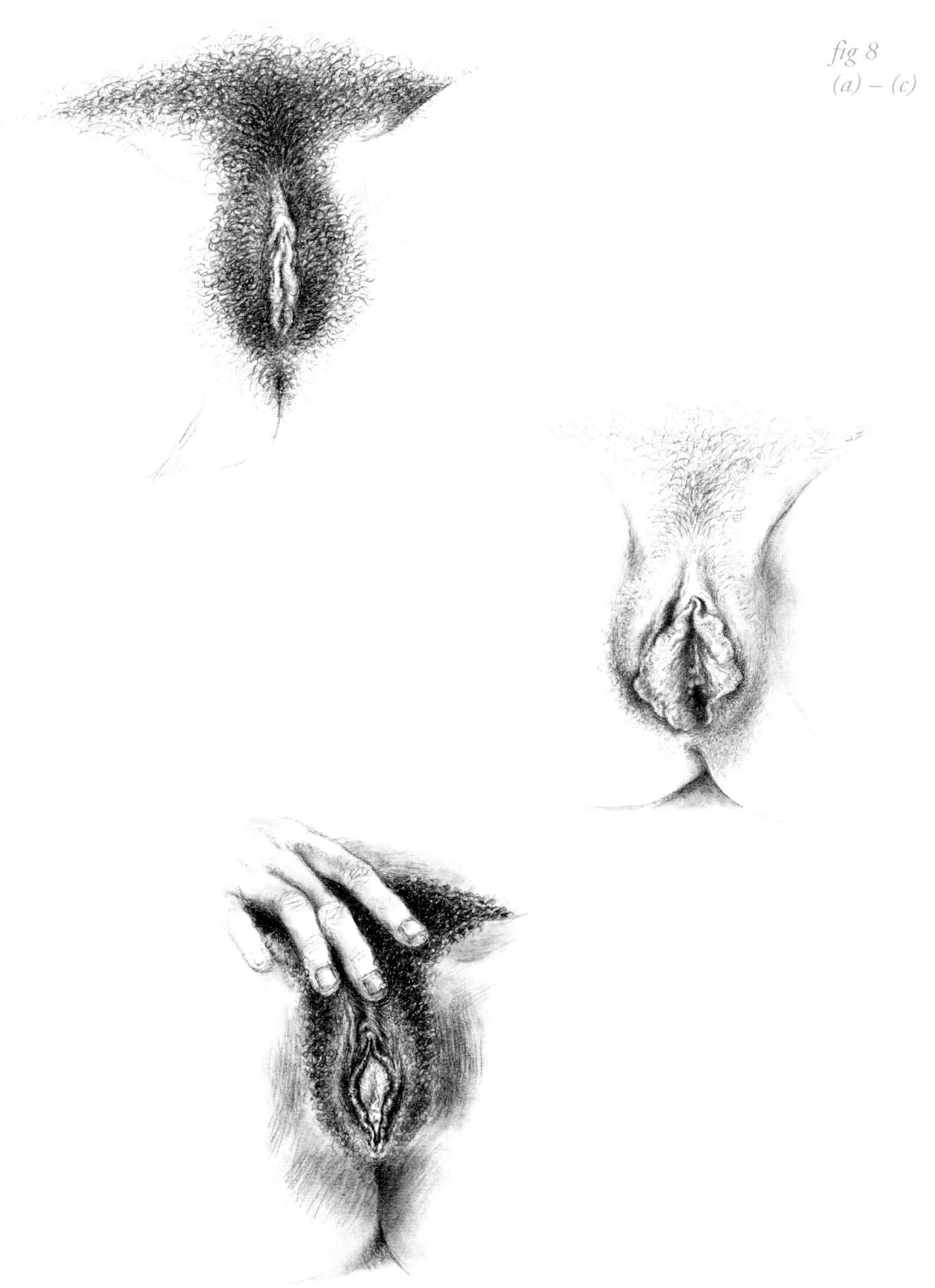

fig 8
(a) – (c)

thick and some are thin. Some are circumcised, some aren't. But they can nearly all do what they were designed to do.

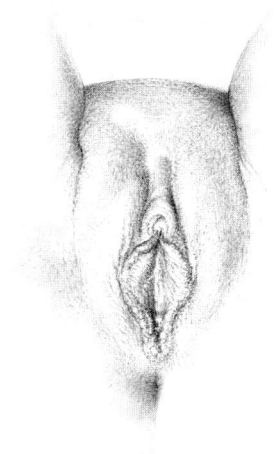

fig 8 (d)

Turning to the vulvas, you'll observe that some are wide-open, some are narrow, some have long lips, some have short ones, some are very hairy and others are not. However, all of them can make a very good job of fucking.

Sometimes, people do have structural abnormalities which cause sex difficulties. By far the commonest example of this is the widening and laxity of the vagina which affects so many women who've had several children. But with medical help, it's usually possible to put matters right (see Chapter Five).

WHAT IS INTERCOURSE?

So what is intercourse? Legally speaking, it's any contact at all between a penis and a vagina. However, in practice it actually involves *penetration* of the vagina by the penis, so that the man's phallus lies inside the woman's 'vaginal cavity'.

Fortunately, a guy's 'prick' is perfectly shaped to fill this cavity (*fig 9*). A cross-section through the penis is like a triangle pointing downwards, but with rounded corners. As you'll observe, that 'inverted triangle' shape exactly matches the opening between the woman's inner lips.

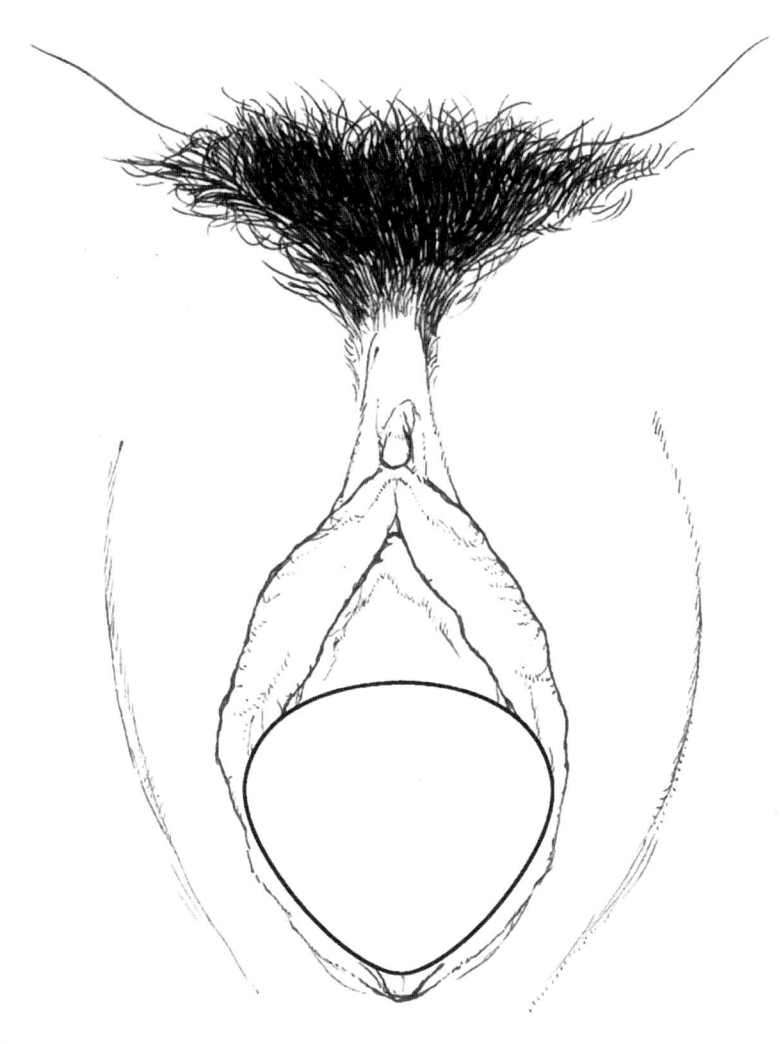

fig 9

Thus, her outer 'collar' should fit very snugly around the base of his column, giving both of them very nice feelings.

What about what goes on *inside*? Well, once more the diagram (*fig 10*) makes it all clear. In this cutaway drawing, the penis is shown filling pretty well all of the vagina – with its tip approaching the woman's cervix.

An important point is that once the man is fully inside, the 'back' of his penis (that's the flat surface which is nearest to him when he's erect) is creating a certain amount of pressure on the woman's G-spot – especially if he leans back a bit.

Recent medical research in Holland has revealed more about what goes on inside the vagina during intercourse. For the first time ever, doctors have been able to look inside the moving bodies of women who were enthusiastically having sex – the object being to find out where the penis was in relation to the female's various genital organs, and what it was doing to them.

How did the Dutch medics achieve this? They asked some gallant couples to indulge in a spot of fucking inside an MRI scanner. (As anyone who has had an MRI scan done will know, this can't have been easy: you have to lie on a cramped bed inside an extremely noisy tunnel while the pictures are taken…)

Anyway, each couple had intercourse in the missionary position, with the *Mijnheer* on top of the *Mevrouw*, of course – and the results were published in the British Medical Journal (*fig 11*). They reveal the surprising fact that, during sexual congress, the penis is usually bent *upwards* – like a banana.

The *tip* of the cock not only presses against the woman's cervix, but also to some extent against her bladder – which explains why it's often a good idea for the woman to go and have a pee beforehand;

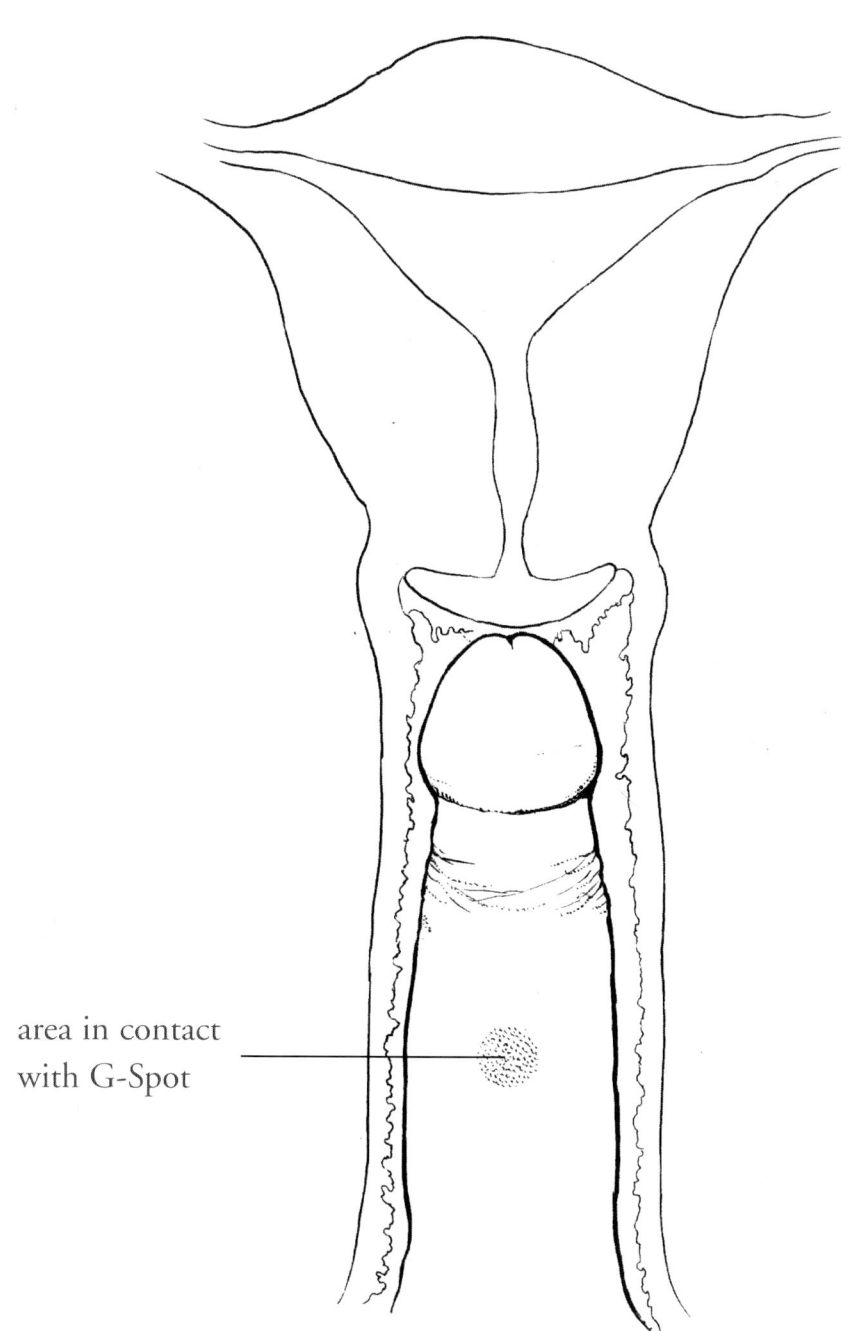

area in contact
with G-Spot

fig 10

in order to create more room in her pelvis, and thus make herself more comfortable. (Nevertheless, some women do sometimes *enjoy* making love with a full bladder, in order to increase pelvic tension and to create a feeling that they might have to 'squirt' at any moment…).

Another thing that the MRI scan reveals is that the hard ridge on the underside of the man's penis presses very firmly against the front wall of his partner's rectum; this pressure is appreciated by the many women who derive strong sexual sensations from the rectal area.

Finally – as you can clearly detect from the scan – the man's testicles do bang against the woman's perineum (the area of skin between her vagina and her anus) as he thrusts into her. Men aren't

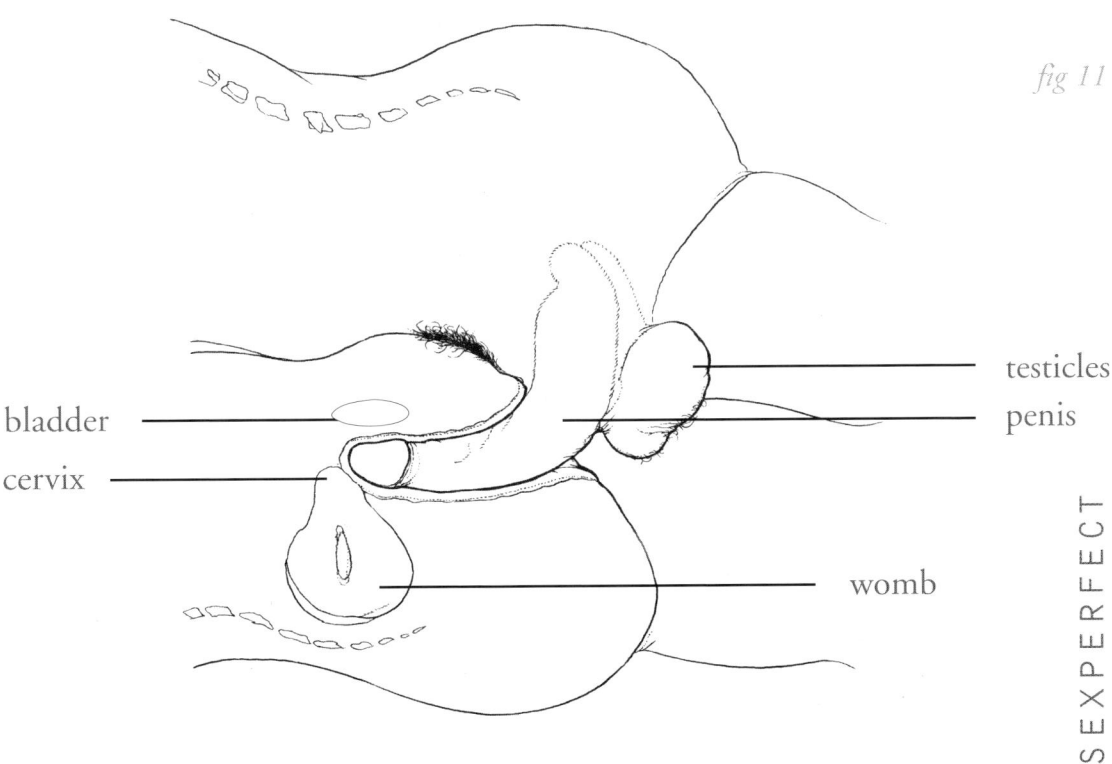

fig 11

testicles

penis

bladder

cervix

womb

generally aware of this happening, but a lot of females like the sensation very much indeed.

BEGINNING INTERCOURSE

When you're ready to penetrate – or be penetrated – what should you do first?

Well, it's important not to charge straight in; as in other fields of life, 'rushing your fences' is likely to be counter-productive. So please take your time…

As a rule, it's a very good move to hold the labia open with your fingers (*fig 12*). Either of you can do this, and it makes the entry of the penis much easier.

And many women – particularly younger ones who've never had babies and are therefore relatively 'narrow' – do appreciate it if the man continues to hold the 'flaps' back until he is in up to the hilt.

WHAT NEXT?

But for the moment, let's assume that the guy is still outside his partner's vagina. See illustrations (*fig 13, 14, 15*) for the process of getting in.

For most couples, the moment of penetration goes pretty well, but there can be difficulties, particularly when a relationship is starting out. Very commonly, it's a bit tricky for the man to assess the exact *angle of tilt* of his new partner's vagina. A good tip is to aim your penis at a point located at the top of her 'bottom cleavage'. That'll usually guide you in the right direction.

Another useful ploy is to use the 'Birmingham Entry Technique'. In this manoeuvre, the woman actually *holds* the man's penis in her

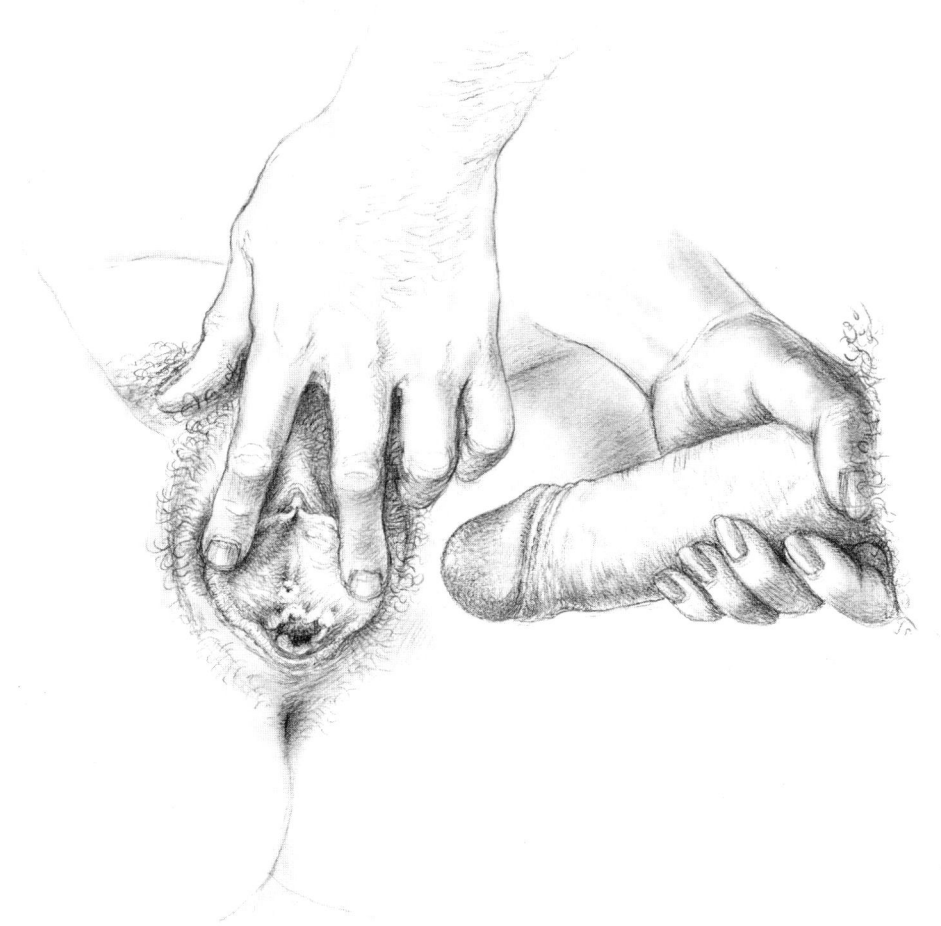

fig 12

hand and guides it in. An advantage of this method is that the firm pressure of her fingers helps to maintain a good erection.

IN AND OUT...

In human males, there is a colossal, instinctual need to drive the penis in and out of the vagina; the same overwhelming urge is, of course, found in other male mammals. Women often have a similar urge to thrust the pelvis back and forth, so as to meet the man's surges.

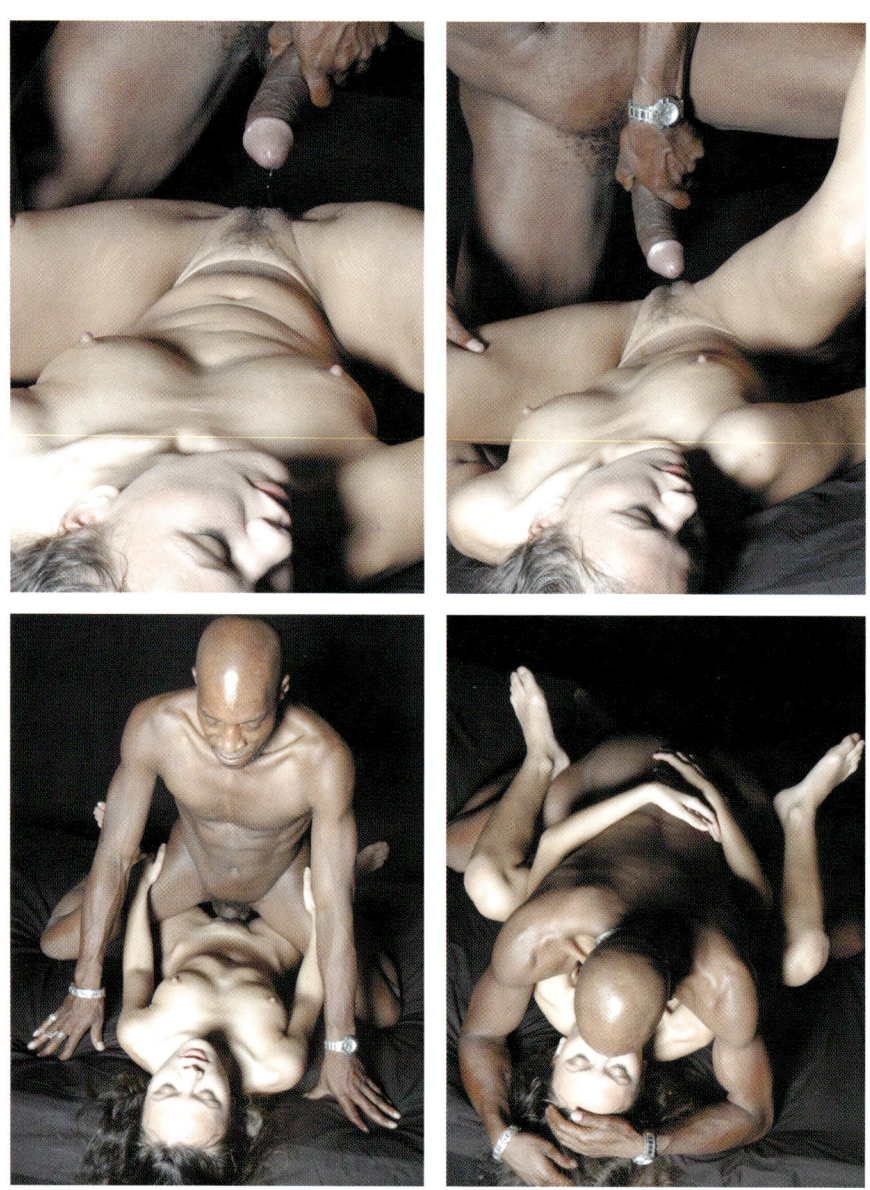

fig 13
fig 14
fig 15
(a) – (b)

fig 15 (c)

All this 'to-ing and fro-ing' has two main purposes:

•   Through friction, to stimulate the erogenous nerve endings in the man's penis and the woman's vagina – and thus give both of them powerful and delightful sensations;

•   Eventually, to produce a climax in the male.

However, every man who is reading this book should bear in mind the vital fact that so many, many men forget: that for women, stimulation of the vagina *alone* is not usually enough. In order to achieve the highest levels of ecstasy, they must also have stimulation of their clitorises. Indeed, without direct stimulation of the clitoris, few women can climax. I've seen many a sexual relationship founder because the male partner would not take this on board!

See Chapter Three for much more about sexual intercourse in relation to the clitoris.

HOW FAST SHOULD YOU GO?

A question I'm frequently asked by email correspondents (particularly young couples) is 'How *fast* should we go?'

Well, there's no recommended rate for thrusting. Research shows that most twosomes do it at a rate of about 60 per minute – speeding up towards the end, of course.

But there is much to be said for *varying* the speed – sometimes pushing in and out at a rate of 30 per minute (the famous 'slow, comfortable screw'), and sometimes upping the rate to a brisk 120.

One word of warning: women should beware of 'High-Speed Harry' – the guy who has seen too many porn films, and has got the idea from them that everything must be done 'at the double.' Harry tries to poke you with a frequency of anything between 150 and 200 thrusts per minute – which is not generally very comfortable (or satisfying) for the woman on the receiving end. He doesn't realise that the reason so many blue video stars go so laughably fast is that they are desperately trying to maintain their erections…

So if in doubt, just ask your partner to tell you how fast she would like it. Finally, don't hesitate to *vary* the rhythm – and depth – of your thrusts. It's a good plan to change the pattern every minute or two.

Remember above all the wise counsel inherent in the famous old limerick:

A handsome young man named McNameter
Had a cock of prodigious diameter;
Yet it wasn't his size
Gave the girls dreamy eyes –
But his rhythm: iambic pentameter!

HOW LONG SHOULD IT LAST?

Now how long should sexual intercourse last?

The short answer is 'for as long as you both want it to.' But please appreciate that men and women do often have rather differing views on this subject.

As a very rough rule of thumb, women tend to want it to continue rather longer than men do. Over the years, I must have had hundreds of letters from younger women who said things like, 'I couldn't *believe* it when he finished so quickly…'

CASE STUDY

Samantha was 18 and a virgin. A gorgeous-looking girl, she was quite afraid of the idea of sexual intercourse – mainly because her mother had told her that sex would be 'very painful.' Some of her friends had hinted to her that the first time hadn't been too good for them either…

So when boys of her own age tried to get her into bed, she kept on turning them down.

But then she got a place at Cambridge, and began to meet other young women who told her that sexual intercourse could be great fun.

Halfway through her third term, she met a male lecturer from another college while she and her pals were punting on the River Cam. He invited her out to dinner, and bought her flowers and perfume. She was quite bowled over by this sophisticated older man especially as her friends hinted that he was known to be very experienced with women, and highly skilled in bed…

When they finally got to his bedroom, she was pleasantly surprised to find that his penis – the first one she'd ever seen – wasn't the huge, threatening thing she had feared, but was actually quite small and manageable!

And his expert foreplay made her so relaxed, comfortable and well-lubricated that when the moment finally came for him to slip his rather attractive penis inside her, she found the experience an unexpected delight.

Samantha has never looked back. She enjoys her sex-life

This reflects the fact that, until quite recent times, the object of the average young male was simply to get his semen into a girl as fast as humanly possible! (Especially if there was a chance that her mum and dad might come home…)

Indeed, as recently as the 1980s there was nationwide astonishment when I published the results of an excellent Caledonian survey which showed that Scotswomen actually wished that intercourse would go on for half an hour. Many British men couldn't accept that this was humanly possible.

Even in France, a newspaper reported the story under the slightly surprised headline:

LES BELLES ECOSSAISES PREFERERAIENT UNE BONNE DEMI-HEURE!

And in the mid-1990s, my associate and I carried out a sex survey among 5,000 national newspaper readers. This revealed that:

- The average feller claimed that intercourse with him usually lasted for over 20 minutes.
- In contrast, the average woman reported that it only lasted for eight minutes!

These days, thanks to the constant – and quite justifiable – campaign by liberated women for More Fun In The Bedroom, the two sexes do seem to be getting on rather more equably where duration of sex is concerned. Most intelligent and loving couples seem to have no real difficulty in agreeing on how long sexual intercourse should last.

But the last piece of advice I would give on this topic is pretty blunt:

A man must *never* finish intercourse until his partner is thoroughly satisfied.

enormously, and she says that she'll always be grateful to the older man who first showed her that intercourse could be a really lovely experience.

TALKING DURING INTERCOURSE

Another big change in recent years has been this: a high proportion of couples used to make love in complete silence (apart from grunts, of course).

But nowadays, most people do *talk* to each other while they're having intercourse. They are much less embarrassed (even in England), and they urge each other on, saying helpful things like:

- 'That's great! Do it again.'
- 'Yes – push it in further.'
- 'Cmon, baby – oh yessss – please give it to me!'
- 'Squeeze my breasts/balls while you do that…'
- And of course, 'OK, hon – I'm ready to come!'

In the main, it's a jolly good idea if the two of you can *communicate* often during sexual intercourse. Don't hesitate to use frank language – unless you think it's the sort that will upset your partner. Fortunately, these days both sexes are often turned on by honest, Anglo-Saxon expressions and will merrily shriek out, at moments of sexual ecstasy, gems such as, 'Oh *fuck*! I really do love *FUCKING*!'

Finally, it may help if I give you a list of a few useful *alternatives* for the word 'fucking' – just in case one of you finds it inappropriate in your bedroom. They are:

- Screwing
- Bonking
- Shagging – much favoured by Sir Richard Burton in his

translations of *The Arabian Nights*, but ceased being used by polite people (apart, of course, from my friend Simon Heffer) until re-introduced by TV comedians in the mid-1990s

- Rogering
- Poking
- Swyving – a Chaucerian word which proved extremely useful back in the 20th Century when 'fuck' could not be printed

That's it – so, Happy Swyving!

intercourse at various angles

Connoisseurs of sexual intercourse will be aware that there are various factors that can make fucking very good indeed.

These include:

- Love
- Tenderness
- Romance
- Skilled foreplay
- And… the *angle* of intercourse

Well, this chapter is about the angle of intercourse.

The precise angle of penetration is of some *medical* importance, because quite often women complain about pain during intercourse – if the angle isn't quite right for them. This could be because they have an unusually sensitive cervix, or because the penis is hitting an ovary. So, if you get deep pain during sex, try changing the angle! (If that doesn't work, then it's vital to have an internal check-up by a doctor.)

Yes, whether you're male or female, the angle at which the penis goes into the vagina can profoundly affect the feelings that you experience. Why? Because different angles create different *pressures* on the penis – and on the vagina.

Trying new angles is particularly important during pregnancy – because an expectant mum may find that the usual angle either doesn't really satisfy her, or causes her actual discomfort. Good positions to experiment with when you are expecting (all of which are described in this chapter or in Chapters Four and Six) include The Spoons, The Chair, Free As Air, Hector's Horse and The Strauss.

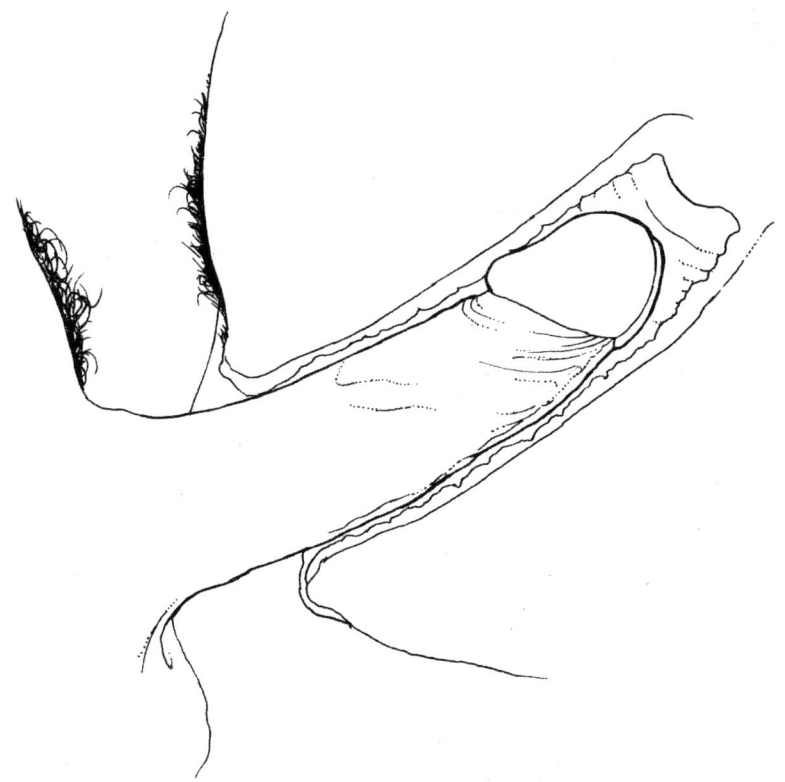

fig 16

Most men already know the dramatic effects that pressure can have on sexual sensations. This is because, through masturbation, they've learned that pressing on different parts of the penis can completely alter what they feel – and even change the entire sensation of a climax. (Indeed, a lot of males say that their most intense orgasms are achieved by pressing on the penile shaft in various ways, just before they come.)

So it's well worth experimenting with various angles of intercourse, so as to see which ones turn you both on. It's not only instructive – it's fun!

THE USUAL ANGLE – THE MISSIONARY POSITION

Let's begin by looking at the *usual* way in which the penis goes into the vagina. The cutaway drawing on the previous page (*fig 16*) of how the man's cock lies when it's fully inside his partner's vaginal channel. Obviously, it's aligned in the same plane as the vagina and although the 'angle of tilt' of the vagina varies a bit from female to female, this agreeable 'love channel' invariably runs upwards and backwards – following a line that is roughly parallel with the woman's rectum. That's why we said in Chapter One that when you're pushing your penis into your partner's vagina for the first time, it's a good idea to direct your tip in the general direction of the topmost part of her buttock cleavage, so as to maximise her comfort.

For instance, one can begin in the famous 'missionary' position – which is far and away the most popular one for couples who are just embarking on a new relationship (*fig 17, 18*).

Our missionary begins by lining up his penis outside the vulva and directing it upwards into his new convert's vagina at approximately the angle we've described (*fig 17*). In the next illustration (*fig 18*), you can see that he has no difficulty at all in slipping it gently into her. Clearly, this is a good start to what is going to be a very happy relationship…

However, once two partners are used to each other, and happy to experiment a little, they can begin trying out different angles.

FACE-TO-FACE STANDING

The next position is a simple variation of angle, suitable for a man and woman who are just getting to know each other's bodies (*fig 19*). They are standing facing each other – a situation in which the man will generally have to bend his knees a trifle. Depending on

fig 17

fig 18

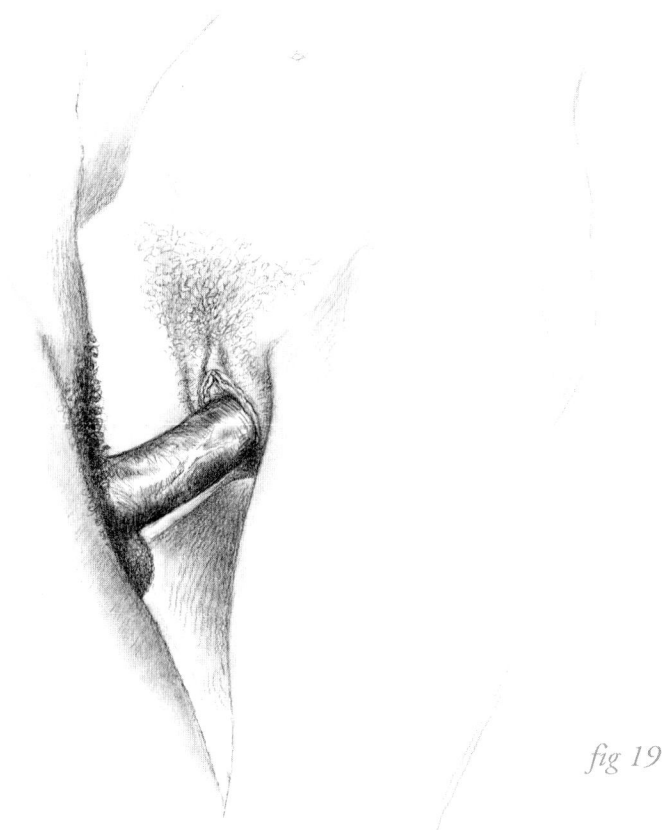

fig 19

how much he bends them, his erect penis will enter her vagina at slightly different angles. And – most importantly – by moving his hips to the left (as in the picture above) or to the right, he can make his shaft press against the *side* walls of her vagina.

REAR-ENTRY

For a dramatic reversal of angle, one can try the rear-entry positions (*fig 20*). The way in which this affects pressures within the vulvo-vaginal area is clearly demonstrated by the accompanying drawing (*fig 21*). Please note that the 'ridge' of the penis is now pressing

fig 20

against the *front* wall of the vagina, rather than the *back* – as happens in standard face-to-face positions. It's also pressing against the front of the vulva – but NOT against the clitoris. As we'll see in Chapter Three, there are – alas – hardly any intercourse positions in which the penis gives direct clitoral stimulation.

Meanwhile, the flat dorsum (back) of the penis is pressing against the rear part of the vulval opening. These factors give the woman quite different sensations from those she enjoys in the missionary position.

And an added bonus is that the penile ridge (often known as the 'pleasure ridge') is, as you'll observe, exposed – and therefore capable of being stimulated by the finger-tips of either party. Not only is this exciting, but it also helps if the guy starts losing his stiffness…

There are numerous variants of the rear-entry position, and they can all substantially alter the angle of penetration of the penis into the vagina. For example, there's the celebrated 'doggy position',

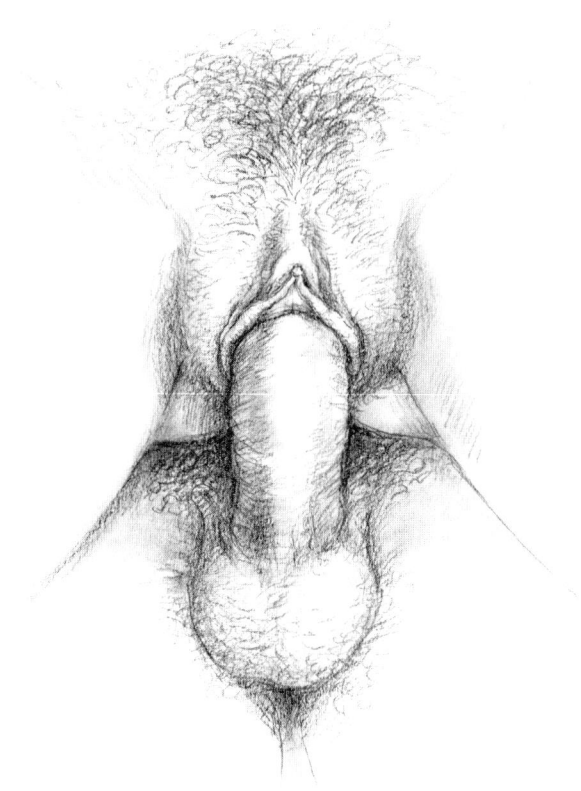

fig 21

which imitates the mating mode of our four-legged friends. A good way of doing it is with the woman on all fours, and the man kneeling behind her (*fig 22*). By moving his body upwards or downwards, or from side to side, the male partner can alter the sensations which his 'mate' experiences – and the ones he feels himself.

Another very useful position is 'the spoons' – so called because the couple lie together like two spoons in a drawer (*fig 23*). Here the

fig 22

man can slip into the woman from behind, being careful not to penetrate her anus by mistake – unless you are ready and want to have anal sex together, that is!

Generally, he'll enter with the tip of his cock pointing forwards against the front wall of her vagina and toward the region of her bladder. Where he reaches depends to some extent on the length of his phallus, but some couples find that it's possible to stimulate the G-spot in this position.

But a better way of stimulating the famous G-spot is to use the position in which the guy is lying flat on his back with his partner kneeling or sitting astride him (*fig 24*). The trick here is for the woman to lean so far backwards that the man's staff has to press against the front wall of her vagina, in the region where the mysterious but erotic 'Graefenberg spot' is located.

I must admit, however, that whatever angle your penis goes in at,

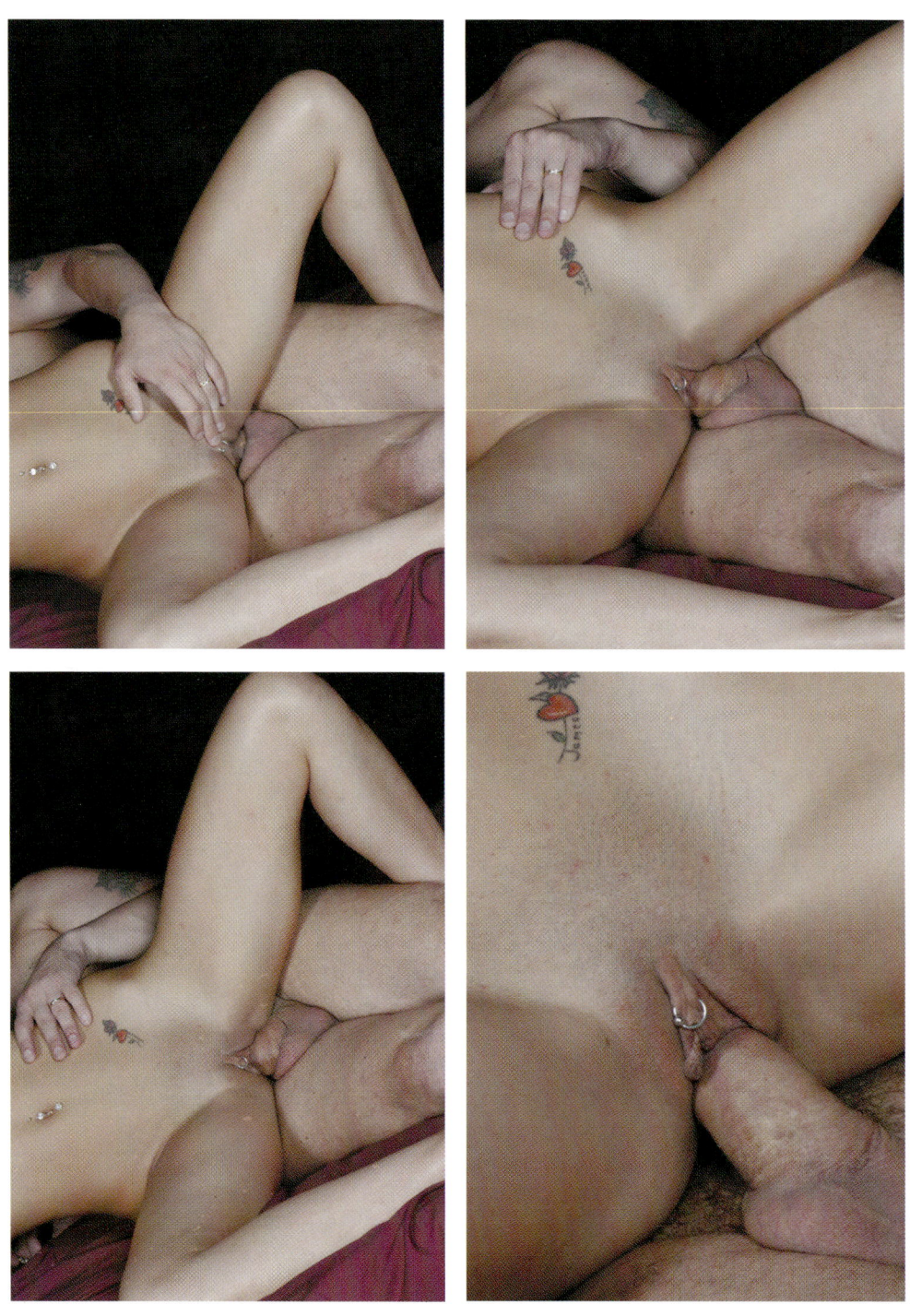

fig 23
(a) – (d)

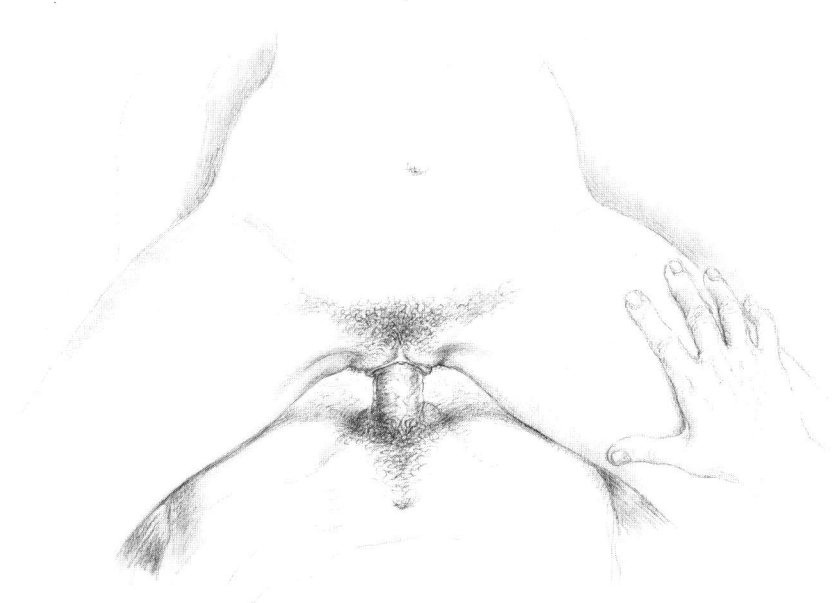

fig 24 (a)

it's unlikely to stimulate the G-spot as efficiently as your fingers can. This is because the G-spot is 'round a corner', behind the woman's pubic bone. So to get at it properly and really drive your loved one to ecstasy, you need something that bends. And your finger bends through over 90 degrees – while your penis *doesn't* (at least, let's hope not).

CUISSADE POSITIONS

A way of producing interesting new sensations for the female partner is the *cuissade* position, so called from the French for 'thigh'

fig 24 (b)

(*cuisse*) because the guy thrusts the upper part of his leg between the woman's thighs (*fig 25*). The idea is that by entering from behind her buttocks, you go into her vagina at a diagonal angle, thus stimulating both the sides and the back of her vagina.

Top British sexpert Rachel Swift maintains that this is 'the most underrated position of them all – one of the greats.' Rachel – a Cambridge don who knows what she is talking about – says in her book *Satisfaction Guaranteed* that the *cuissade* (a.k.a. 'the starfish') has a host of advantages for women – because it's comfortable, because the woman doesn't have to take any weight on her tummy, and because it 'allows the woman easy access to her own parts; she can rub herself, even without the man knowing.'

To which I would simply add that in this posture, the man also has 'easy access to her parts.' And if he rubs them *properly*, she definitely *will* know…

FLANQUETTE POSITION

Closely related to the *cuissade* position is the *flanquette* (*fig 26*). Again, the man puts his thigh between hers. But here, he is approaching the vagina from the *front*, rather than the back.

fig 25

CASE STUDY

Verity was one of my favourite patients. She was a beautiful, witty, amusing girl of 18 – and she had the world's most boring fiancé.

One day, she came into my consulting room and complained that, "Sex with him just isn't doing anything for me, doctor."

She revealed that her partner – a dull 'anorak' of a man – always insisted on making love in the same position. Invariably, it was the missionary.

She didn't find this angle of entry either comfortable or satisfying. And of course, it did absolutely nothing for her clitoris…

She was about to go on holiday to the South of France with a girl friend. And she asked me whether she thought she would have any better luck if she tried having sex with someone else while she was away.

I told her quite frankly that I thought there was every chance that she would – so I provided her with contraception, and also some advice about safe sex.

At the Hotel Negresco in Nice, she met a dashing Provencal artist, and went to bed with him. He made love to her at all sorts of different angles, and in all sorts of positions – paying particular attention to what he called her 'leetle English clicli ' (clitoris). Needless to say, she had a wonderful time.

She now lives in Provence, with her husband and two children. You will not be surprised to hear that the man she chose to marry was not 'the anorak'.

The effect is that your penis enters her vagina at a slantwise angle, so that it stimulates both the sides and the front of her vagina. Your thigh presses against her clitoral area, and it's also fairly easy for either of you to rub her clitoris with your fingers.

THE CLITORIS

That last point is of massive importance. As I said earlier in this chapter, hardly any intercourse positions – no matter what the angle of entry of the penis – provide adequate stimulation of the clitoris by the penis.

So, if you are to bring your lover to climax after climax during sexual intercourse, you *must* find other ways of exciting her clitoris (an organ now thought to be far more extensive and complex than hitherto).

All is revealed in the next chapter…

fig 26

intercourse and the clitoris

The 'CAT' – and the 'Pussy'
Bouncing in off the Clitoris
Frigging her with the Penis

This is the most important chapter in the book – because it deals with the secret of female pleasure: the clitoris.

Recently, there's been a lot of discussion of the clitoris in the media – thank heavens! I say 'thank heavens' because it used to be a forbidden subject; as late as 1997, many magazines and newspapers simply wouldn't print the word 'clitoris'. The change has mainly occurred because of the widely-reported 1998 researches of Dr Helen O'Connell, in Melbourne – which appear to show that the clitoris is a much bigger organ than previously thought. If you're squeamish, just skip the next few lines! Dr O'Connell carried out anatomical dissections on the bodies of a number of elderly women, and found that the clitoris seems to extend a long way internally – with projections wrapping themselves round the vagina and the urinary pipe. This may explain why pressure on these areas often causes intense pleasure.

Unfortunately, from the point of view of a male's ability to supply pleasure, there is a very slight 'design fault' in the otherwise wonderful anatomy of a woman. It's this. *The clitoris is located more than an inch above the point where the penis enters the vagina.*

Now the result of this is that – as a general rule – the male organ is most unlikely to stimulate the clitoris during sexual intercourse. There are actually some ways of getting round that, as we'll see in a moment. But basically, a penis which is inside a vagina cannot rub against a clitoris.

As you can clearly see from the next illustration (*fig 27*), the man's shaft is driving into the woman's vaginal opening – but even the very uppermost part of that shaft is nowhere near her clitoris. Therefore:

- She will NOT enjoy intercourse fully
- She will NOT get delirious with excitement
- She will almost certainly NOT reach orgasm

The implications of this are enormous. You see, my postbag is full of letters from men who say things like:

> 'Dear Doctor Delvin,
> My girl friend is stunningly beautiful, but although we have intercourse three times a week, it never makes her climax. Is she frigid?'

To which the answer is: of course she isn't. What is wrong is that the *young* man (and it's usually a young man) is making the classic male mistake of thinking that women should reach orgasm through intercourse alone. Alas, most females *cannot* do this!

It's quite understandable that so many men think that sexual intercourse alone should be enough to make a woman come. After all, a high proportion of the male population has read those rather naïve pornographic stories in which all the heroines invariably climax at the drop of a hat…

These yarns usually go something like this:

> 'Without wasting any time on foreplay, Horatio rammed his magnificent organ into the fair Jemima. Only ten seconds later, she was already gasping with desire. And when – half a minute after that – he spurted his load into her pink passage, she immediately went into the most devastating orgasm he had ever seen…'

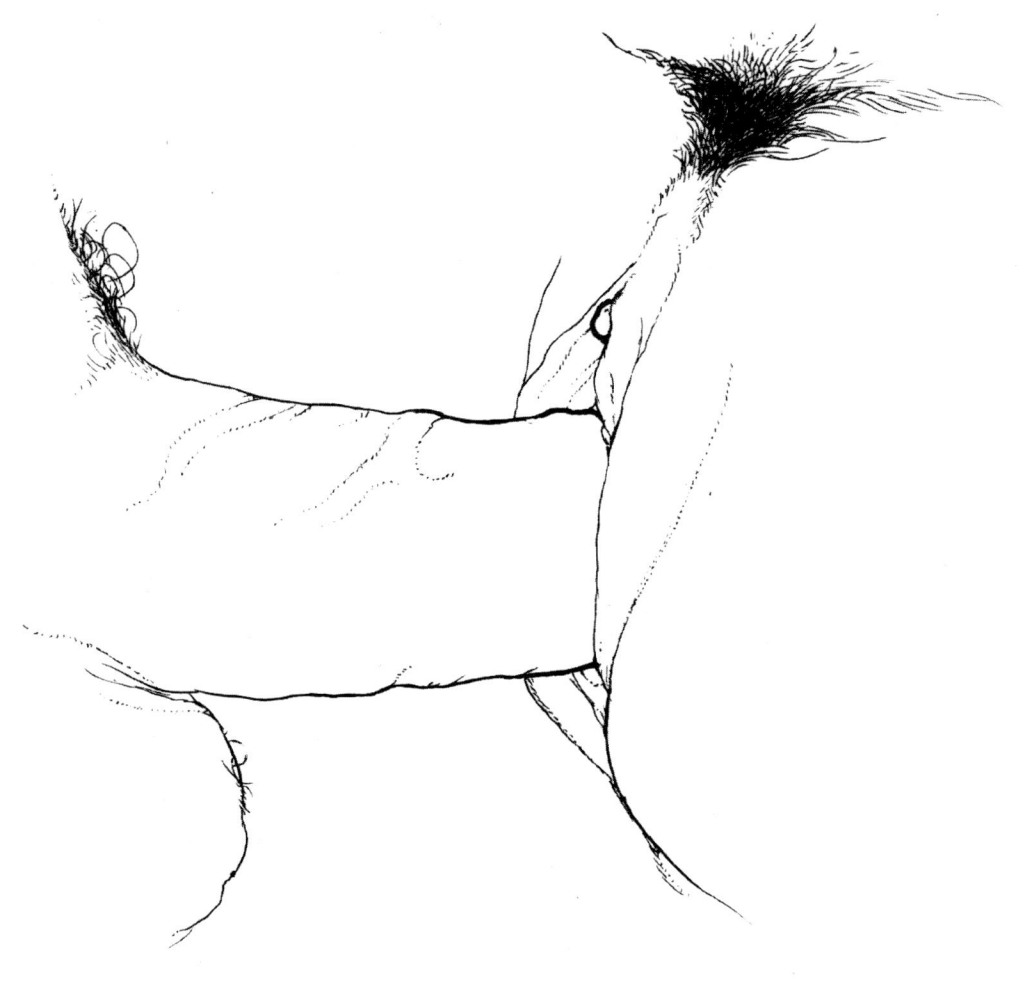

fig 27

Gosh, what fun! But of course the above paragraph is simply *full* of the grossest misunderstandings about female sexuality. We'll deal with all of them later in this book. But for the moment, let's concentrate on the simple fact that ordinary intercourse does not stimulate the clitoris.

For completeness' sake, I should add that the great American sexologists Masters and Johnson – who influenced many people's thinking about sexual matters in the 1970s and 1980s – said authoritatively that intercourse 'tugs' on the vaginal lips, and that this 'tugging' gives some indirect stimulus to the clitoris. That is probably true in some cases.

However, the vital practical point is this: *most women will not climax unless somebody stimulates their clitorises – directly*. Men neglect this point at their peril.

So what can a loving couple do in order to make sure that the woman's clitoris is adequately stimulated during fucking? Well, these are the options for my male readers:

• Choose a position in which your fingers can get to her clitoris while you penetrate her – this is explained in the next chapter, which is about hand-play

• Choose a position in which *her* fingers can do the clitoral frigging – again, see the next chapter

• While you are bonking her, wear or use a sex aid that stimulates her clit – see Chapter Five

• Alter your position to the 'CAT' or the 'Pussy' – of which more in a moment

• Use your cock to masturbate her clit actively during intercourse – I'll show you how at the end of this chapter

THE 'CAT' – AND THE 'PUSSY'

So what are the positions in which the penis can – just about – achieve some pressure on the clitoris? There are two of them: the 'CAT' and the 'Pussy'.

THE 'CAT'

The letters 'CAT' stand for 'Coitally Adjusted Technique'. This position was invented in America, way back in the Clinton era – though whether the President himself used it is uncertain.

The idea was to develop a position in which the penile shaft could come into contact with the clitoral area – by moving the man's body up the bed. In other words, his trunk has to be far higher (relative to the woman's) than normal.

In the next illustration (*fig 28*) you will observe that the woman is lying flat on her back, while the gent is on top of her. But… he has made a real effort to get his head and shoulders about six inches (15cm) nearer to the headboard than usual. So, he is 'riding' much higher up his partner than he usually would.

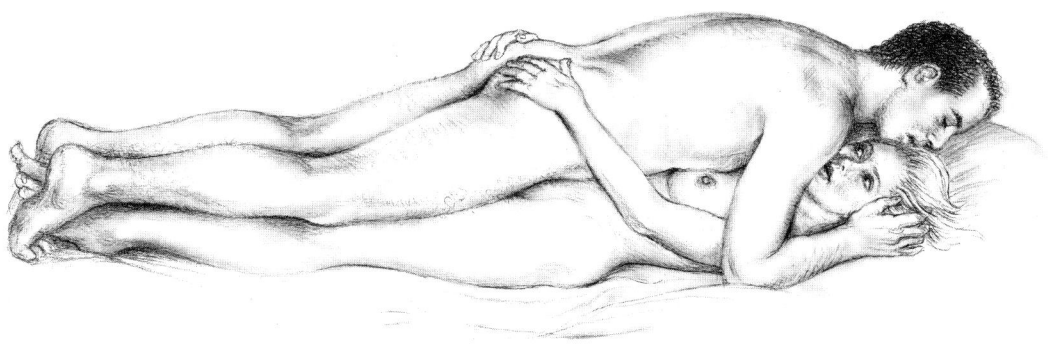

fig 28

The effect of this is to pull the root of his penis upwards – so that, with a bit of luck, it may actually just about touch the clitoris.

Now this means that his penis won't go as far into the vagina as usual. Indeed, you may find that it 'pops out' from time to time. Irritating though that may be to the male partner, the fact is that his girlfriend may well appreciate the contact between the dorsum (back) of his cock and the area round her clitoris.

There's less chance of the penis coming out if the woman keeps her legs together – as you can see (*fig 28*).

Despite the fact that there are no female orgasmic guarantees, quite a lot of couples like the 'CAT', especially in America. It isn't everybody's cup of tea, but it's certainly worth a try to see if it suits you.

THE 'PUSSY'

In contrast, the 'Pussy position' (*fig 29*) was not invented by anyone even remotely connected with the Clinton administration. It was actually thought up by me and my intrepid research partner and it's really just an inversion of the 'CAT' position: the bloke lies flat on his back, with the woman on top. But once again, the vital point is that his head has to be far further up the bed than hers.

If her mouth is roughly on a level with his nipples, then you've got it about right.

As before, the general effect of this arrangement is that the root or base of the penis is pulled up hard against the topmost part of the vaginal opening and, one hopes, against the clitoris.

Believe me: sometimes it works!

fig 29

BOUNCING IN OFF THE CLITORIS

There's another way in which you can stimulate the clitoris as a part of intercourse – and that's to do it directly with the tip of the penis.

Yes, this is possible. However, it demands considerable skill – and practice.

How can you achieve it?

Well, you use the manoeuvre shown in *fig 30*. This demonstrates how the man can gently 'bounce off' the clitoris as he enters the vagina. Indeed, if his partner expresses her pleasure at the feeling this produces (e.g. by saying 'Oooh – *lovely*!'), he can do it again and again – withdrawing his cock and then *lovingly and caressingly* pushing the tip back against the clitoris as he re-enters.

There are those who have criticised this technique as 'bedtime pole-vaulting'!

Nonetheless, it can work very well, and it *has* brought many women to orgasm.

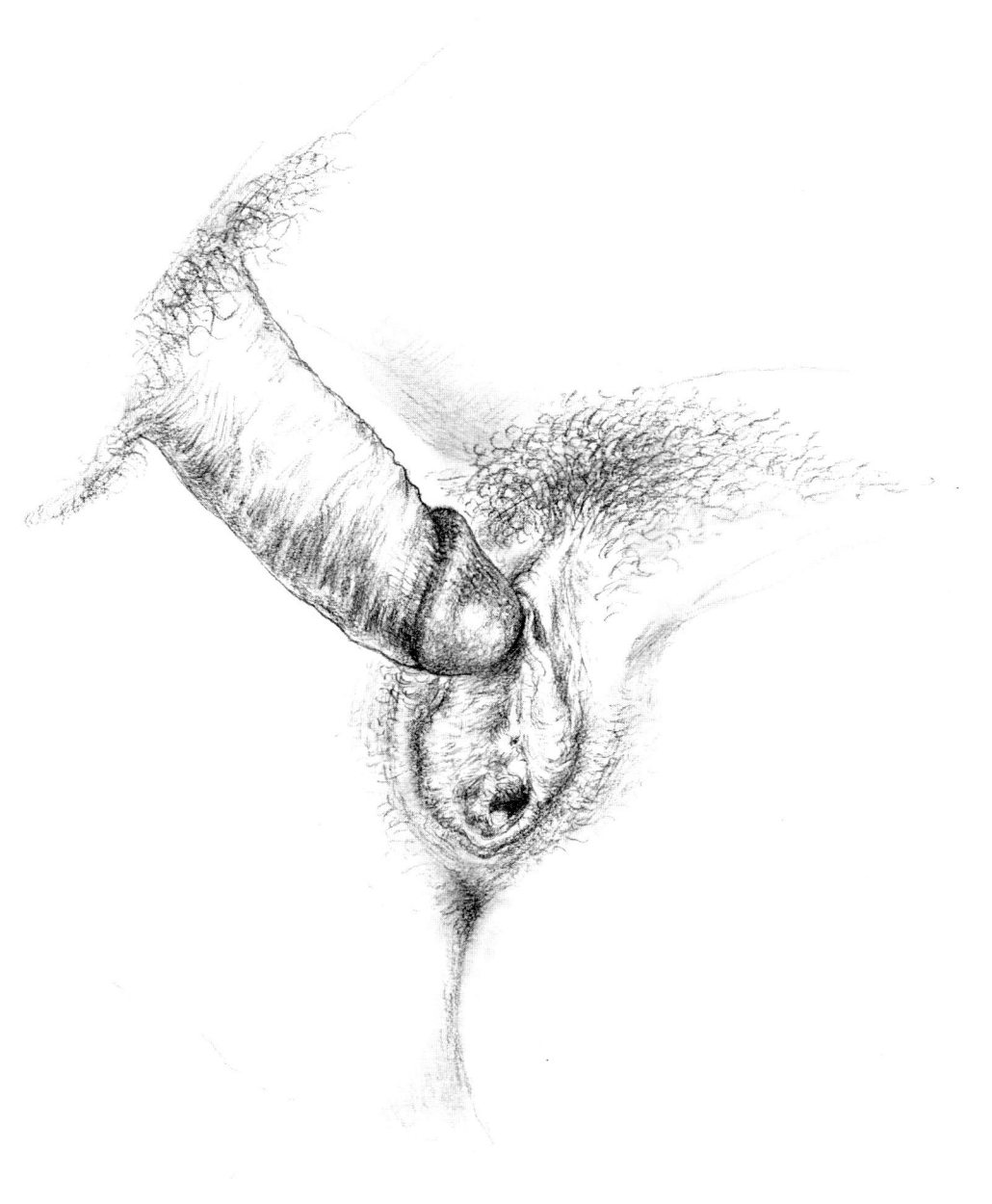

fig 30

FRIGGING HER WITH THE PENIS

Now here's a further solution that is known to very few people. I modestly call it 'the Delvin manoeuvre'. I have taught this technique to dozens of my patients – and nearly all of these couples have

fig 31

found it a very helpful way of aiding the woman to reach orgasm during intercourse.

Basically, it's a simple trick: using the penis as a hand-held dildo!

What you do is take the penis out from time to time during sexual intercourse, hold it in your hand – and use it on the clitoris, much as you would use a vibrator. There are two ways of doing this:

Here (*fig 31*), as you see, it's the *man's* hand that is holding the penis – and he's using it like a sort of sex toy on his partner's clitoris. He's rubbing it against her and – of course – getting her extremely excited. Soon he'll plunge it back inside her. But whenever she needs more stimulation, he will take it out and gently 'rub her up' with it.

And now, it's the *woman's* hand that holds the penis – and which happily uses it as a self-stimulating device (*fig 32*). When she decides that she has had enough stimulation, she will simply pop it back in again.

If she feels like it, she can actually

CASE STUDY

Ruth and Jonathan were a lovely couple. Everybody liked them – despite the fact that they were both lawyers!

There was only one problem in their otherwise happy life: Ruth had the greatest of difficulty in reaching a climax during sexual intercourse. Sometimes she could do it during foreplay. And on days when she was on her own, and got really frustrated, she could easily do it by masturbating.

But during intercourse – no way… absolutely no way.

Many couples would have been perfectly happy with this situation. But Ruth really wanted to come with her beloved Jonathan inside her. So, they asked me for my advice. And I explained to them about how to use the penis to stimulate the clitoris.

That night, Jonathan and Ruth went to bed together. She took charge of things, as female lawyers often do.

When they had made love for a little while, she laid him flat on his back and knelt astride him. Stripped naked and sexually aroused, she must have been a magnificent sight indeed! She put his penis inside her, and began to thrust her lithe hips at him.

Before long, she had driven him nearly wild with excitement. Next, she took his male organ in her right hand – and began to masturbate it vigorously against her clitoris, thus stimulating both of them to even greater heights. When the two of them were ready to climax, she gave three or four more enthusiastic rubs, and finally thrust

fig 32

bring herself off in this way. She can do this as many times as she wishes. What very often happens is that at some point she frigs herself to the very brink of a really shattering climax – and then plunges him inside at the very last second, so that she can enjoy the feeling of coming with him inside her.

The astonishing thing about this technique is that the hand-held penis makes such an excellent dildo, whether it is the man or the woman manipulating it. With its curiously subtle blend of hardness and velvety softness, it is in fact the ideal instrument for stimulating the clitoris – and usually more successful than any vibrator!

However, there are also exciting things you can do with your *hands*.

his penis into her waiting vagina.

Moments later, they both came at the very same instant. It was the first time in her life that she had ever reached orgasm with a man's cock deep inside her.

So it was quite a night for them. And believe me, that was only the beginning...

hand play during intercourse

Things that a Man can do to his
Woman with his Fingers
Things that a Woman can do to
her Man with her Fingers

THINGS THAT A MAN CAN DO TO HIS WOMAN WITH HIS FINGERS

As we've seen, the vital thing that any man who wants to be a skilled lover must know is this: *to give your woman satisfaction during intercourse, you must, must, and must find a way of stimulating her clitoris.*

In the last chapter, we looked at ways of doing it with your penis – quite difficult to start with, but far from impossible.

However, most of the love play that goes on during sexual intercourse is, of course, carried out with the *hands*. And for fairly obvious reasons, much of the hand play that goes on between skilled lovers is directed towards the clitoris.

So in this chapter we're chiefly going to concentrate on things that the two of you can do with your hands to make sure that the clitoris gets adequate attention. But at the very end, we'll run through a number of things that the woman can do for her man – using her hands.

Now there is one big problem that every man has to cope with when he's intending to stimulate his lover's clitoris during the course of coition. It's this. *Your wrist doesn't really bend the right way.*

Let me explain what I mean. If you're a man, imagine yourself facing a beautiful woman, kissing her lovely lips and happily sliding your organ into hers. Now imagine that you're reaching down with your hand, which is squeezed tightly between her belly and yours, so that it's heading for her pubes.

When it reaches the level of her vulva – at which point it will be more or less jammed in between the two of you – what do you find? Your hand is almost certainly facing the wrong way!

fig 33

Here's the problem: unless you're double-jointed, the only comfortable position for your exploring hand is *with the palm facing towards you*. If you try to twist it round so that your palm is fully facing her vulva, you'll find it quite uncomfortable. It may even creak! Why? Because the human wrist just isn't designed to rotate that far! (Incidentally, this is why so many well-intentioned cricket and tennis shots go wrong – but that's another matter.)

fig 34

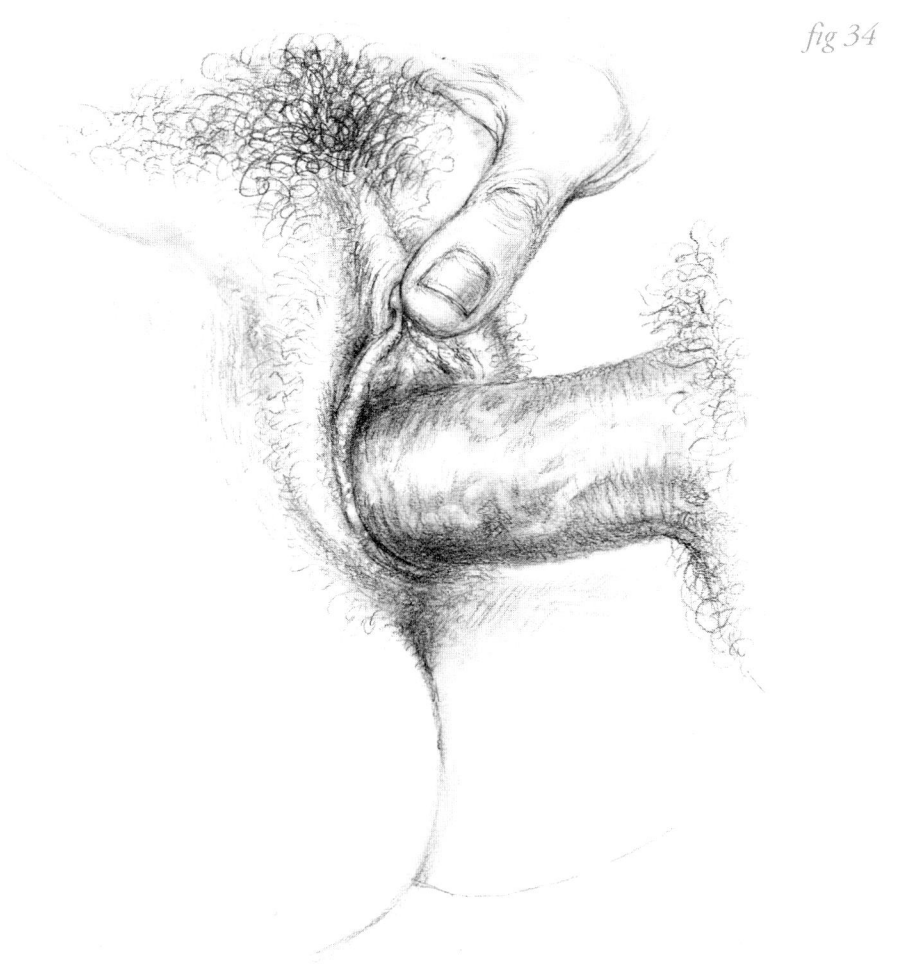

Now is it really of that much importance that getting your hand to face towards her pussy is so awkward? Well, yes it is.

You see, in order to stimulate a woman's labia and clitoris, you need to do it with the soft *pads* of your fingers. In other words, you have to use the 'palm' side of your hand. (It is just about possible to stimulate the clitoris with the hard 'knuckle' side of your fingers – but it isn't easy.)

From the photograph (*fig 33*) you can see that the man and woman are standing facing each other while having intercourse, and he is *trying* to get his hand into the right position to stimulate her clit properly. However, he's having trouble doing it – and is only managing it because she's standing well back from him. If he were lying on top of her, it would be nearly impossible. For anyone with arthritis of the wrist – forget it!

So what can be done about this? Well, one possibility is for the man to use the pad of his *thumb* on his lover's clitoris (*fig 34*). He can do this without breaking his wrist or aggravating his rheumatism! It isn't all that easy to start with – but it can very successfully bring a woman to orgasm during intercourse.

An easier answer is simply *for the woman to do the stimulation of the clitoris herself*!

This makes considerable sense, because her hand actually faces the right way (*fig 35*). He is on top of her, with his penis inside her, but her fingers have plenty of space and are ideally situated for 'self-frigging'. Yes, as many a young girl has discovered for herself, if she drops her hand down toward her groin, her finger tips are automatically curved into the perfect position for stimulating her clitoral 'bud'.

It's easy for the woman to bring any of her fingers into erotic

fig 35

fig 36

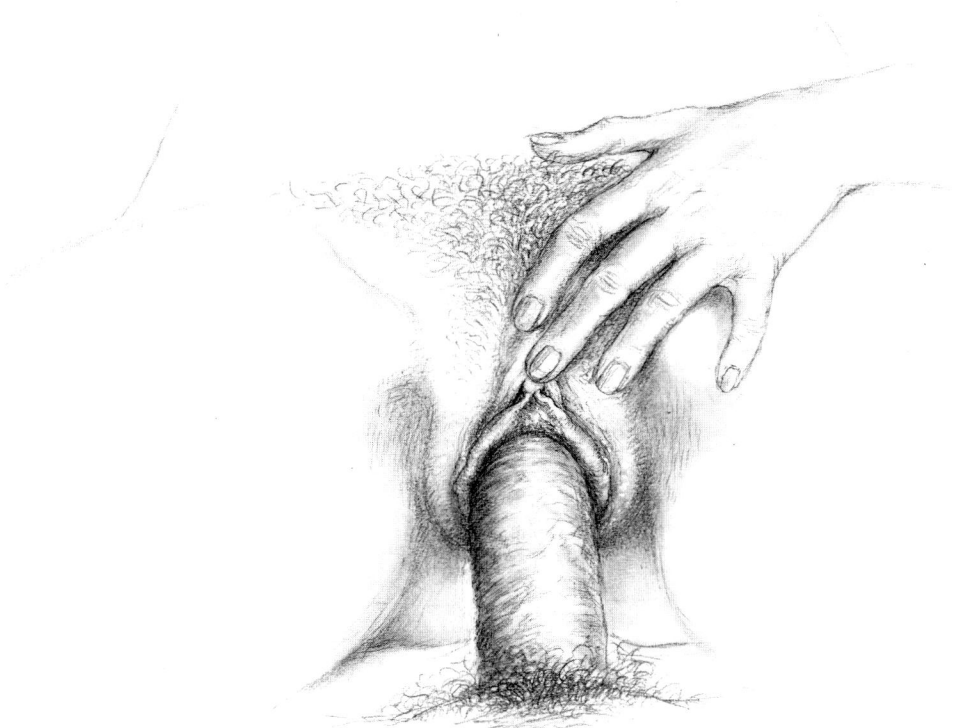

fig 37 (a)

action on her clitoris during sexual intercourse (*fig 36*). It is actually easier for her in a position like the one shown, where the girl is sitting astride the guy's erect cock, while he lies back and enjoys it.

But there are other positions that make it very easy for *either* of the partners to get their fingers onto the clitoral area. For example, a rear-entry position conveniently gives the man easy access to the clitoris (*fig 37*). I strongly recommend this position to any couple having difficulty in achieving female orgasm during coitus.

Similarly, if a man is fucking his partner from behind in a standing position he can simply reach round and bring her off – again and again, if she wishes… (*fig 38*).

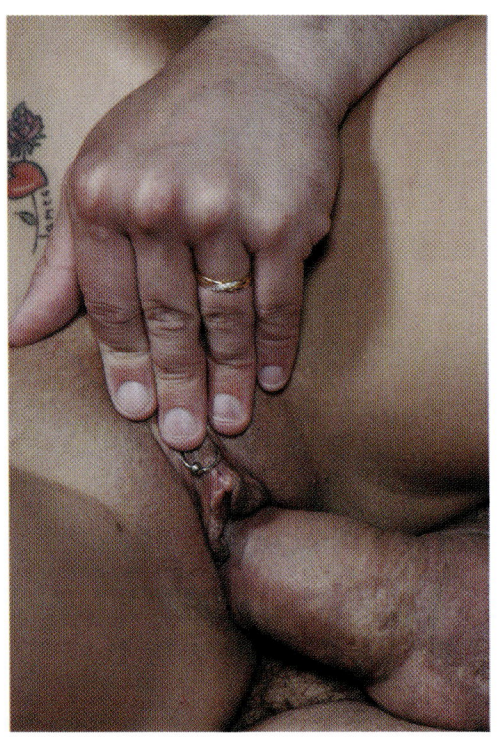

fig 37 (b)

The Chair position demonstrates how a comfortable armchair can be a real boon to a loving couple (*fig 39*). She is sitting sideways across his lap, and her thighs are wide apart so that he can enter her easily. Thus he has a delightfully open access to her clitoris. He can even *see* it – so there's a reasonable chance that he won't get lost (at least, not on this occasion…).

Another good position which gives excellent access to the breasts and to the clitoris is the Free As Air position (*fig 40*). The man lies flat on his back, and the woman lies on *her* back, on top of him.

He enters her from behind, though he'll probably need some assistance from her hands to get him in – and maybe to help him stay in too! But as long as his arms are reasonably long, he should be able to reach her clitoris – and rub it.

So why is it called Free As Air? Simply because it gives the woman complete freedom to stimulate any part of her body she wants to, including her nipples and her clitoris.

Also giving both parties excellent access to the clitoris is the *Cuissade* position, which we discussed in Chapter Two (Intercourse at Various Angles). This is the one in which the man approaches the woman from behind, but with his thigh thrust between hers. A

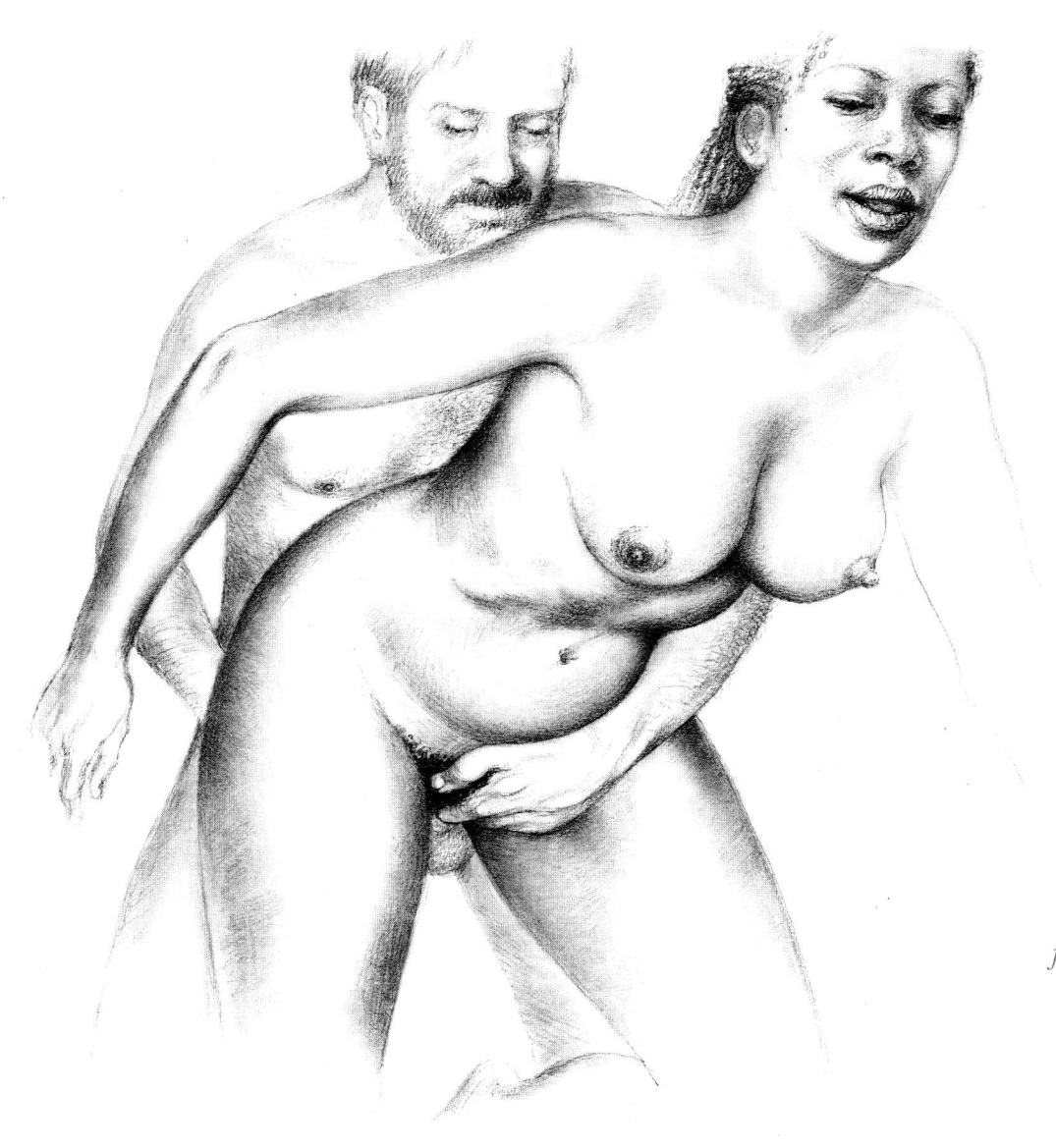

fig 38

fig 39

fig 40

woman who is in the *Cuissade* position can show her partner just exactly where she wants to be touched (*fig 41*).

Finally, I would strongly recommend the Hector's Horse position, which has helped a lot of women to reach orgasm during intercourse. Students of *The Iliad* have so far been unable to determine precisely why this position is named after the Homeric hero (or rather, after his horse). But anyway, there's no doubt that the position works (*fig 42*).

To get into it, the woman should place her man flat on his back on the bed with his knees bent, then kneel astride him and put him inside. Your clitoris and your labia are now entirely visible to him, so he can stroke them in whatever fashion you wish. Or – like the cheery young lass in the picture – you can simply touch yourself up.

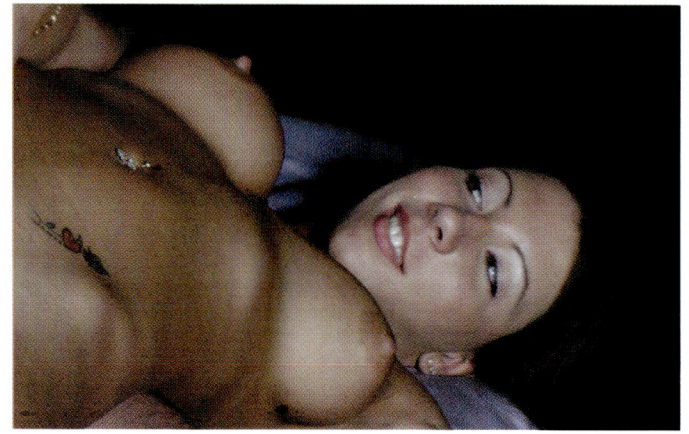

fig 41
(a) – (b)

THINGS THAT A WOMAN CAN DO TO HER MAN WITH HER FINGERS

So as you see, there are many ways in which a man can stimulate his lover's clitoris during intercourse. And believe me, boys, she will be *very* grateful – for the most common complaint that women make about men is the fact that they are all too often neglectful of the 'clit'.

But there are also things that the female can do for the male with her hands during coitus. Here are some of them:

• 'Anal play' (*postillionage*) – this is dealt with in Chapter Eight

• Pinching and caressing his nipples – many men find this very exciting

• Stroking his neck and ears

• Putting your fingers in his mouth – can be very sexy indeed and many couples are really turned on by it

• Holding his balls: most men like it if the woman holds or strokes

CASE STUDY

Victoria was 35, and a successful and stylish businesswoman. For some years, she had 'played the field' with good-looking men whom she met on her trips to cities around the world.

But again and again, the men – charming though many of them were – hadn't really satisfied her. All too often, these couplings were a bit hurried, and the guy had to rush to get a plane or a train before he could really get to work on her body. So serious finger-play was very rare...

Then on a business trip to New York, she met Sylvie – a long-legged South American ballerina who was – like Victoria – staying at the Algonquin Hotel. They had dinner there together, and found themselves getting on like a house on fire. Not altogether surprisingly, they went back to Sylvie's room for drinks – and ended up kissing each other and then falling into the big bed in each other's arms.

During that long night, Sylvie taught Victoria the secrets of love-play with the fingers. And very importantly, she showed her how easy it is for a passionate woman to bring herself off while being hugged and kissed by someone else.

From then on, Victoria's love-life changed. She still 'cherry-picked' delectable males to take to bed. But she made sure that she always reached an orgasm – or indeed a series of orgasms – by using her own fingers. Sylvie had taught her that it's particularly easy to do this when you lie flat on your face – and let the man have sex with you from behind.

In that position, he can't actually see what you're doing – which is quite a good idea if he (poor fellow) is a little bit insecure about female sexuality and can't handle a woman playing with herself during sex.

But, as Sylvie had correctly forecast, many of Victoria's lovers were extremely turned on by the idea of a beautiful, independent-minded woman using her slim, elegant fingers to bring herself off during intercourse.

the scrotum during intercourse – but do take it easy, because squeezing the balls can cause *pain* (and men can be pretty nervous about this!)

• Stroking his penis: in those positions where the penis is partially *outside* your vagina, you may find it helpful to stroke or squeeze his shaft – this is particularly easy when he is making love to you from behind. But bear in mind that over-enthusiastic rubbing may make him come too soon; nonetheless, skilful rubbing can be very useful if your man tends to lose his erection!

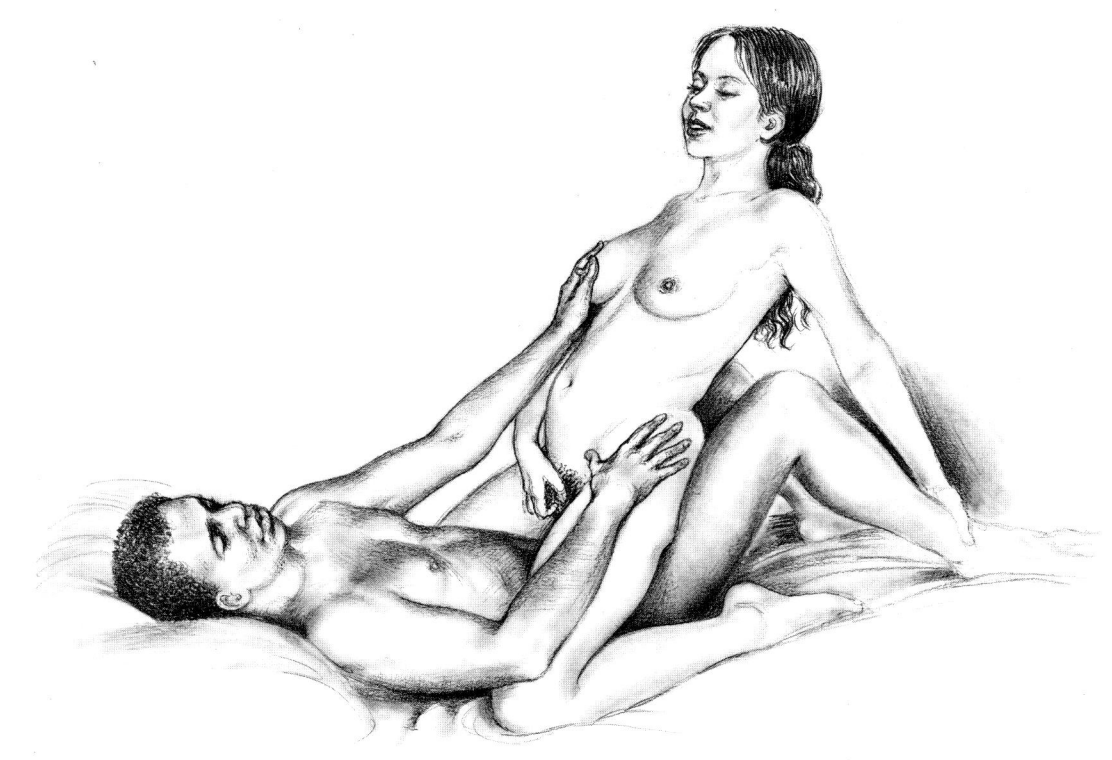

fig 42

sex aids

during

intercourse

Sex aids are here to stay. Although some people are still a little distrustful of them – or think that they bring an 'artificial' flavour to love-making – the fact is that they have helped millions of couples world-wide.

From my own medical experience, I can assure you that they are often useful for:

- Women who are lacking in libido
- Women who have trouble reaching a climax
- Men who have problems with erection
- Men who have difficulty reaching a climax

However, the other important thing about sex aids is this. *They can be great fun – particularly for women, but also for men.*

And in this chapter, we're going to look at ways in which you can use them during sexual intercourse, in order to provide a lot of fun (as well as sexual satisfaction) for you and your partner.

Incidentally, many women – and some men – still feel embarrassed about buying sex aids. There's no need to be. These days, if you don't want to visit a sex shop (or don't have one near you) it's very easy to buy these goods by mail order. (*Editor's note*: the Erotic Print Society can supply you with most of the sex toys discussed by Dr Delvin: see the back of this book for details of how to contact us or receive the free EPS catalogue).

Now what types of sex aid can you use during intercourse?

There are three basic kinds:

- Dildos and vibrators
- Massagers and probes

- Things to wear on the penis

Let's have a look at them in turn:

DILDOS AND VIBRATORS

DILDOS

A dildo is an artificial penis. Dildos (or dildoes) have been manufactured for centuries; indeed, during Charles II's rule, some poor devil got thrown into the Tower for trying to import about 350 of them. Fortunately, that sort of legal action against dildo-smugglers ceased to happen – at least in Britain – around about 1975.

Dildos have traditionally been made in the Orient, where they were carved skilfully out of wood, and then painted to resemble a penis. But these days, they're usually made of coloured plastic – and they can be astonishingly realistic.

There are various reasons for using a dildo. For instance, a guy who loses his erection may wish to continue stimulating his girl with one of these little devices – until such time as he gets it back again. Also, certain women do rather like the idea of being in bed with two penises…

Some couples like to use a small dildo on the clitoris while they're having sex. And – though male readers may find this surprising – there are mature women who have largish vaginas and who like to have a small dildo inside *at the same time as the penis*, in order to get more bulk. (For more about this useful technique, see the section on vibrators on the following pages.)

So dildos have a long and louche history. But in practice, traditional dildos have shrunk to only a minor part of the sex toy market in recent years because of the advent of electrically-powered vibrators.

VIBRATORS

Vibrators are now fantastically popular. They were almost unknown in the Western world until about 1970. At the time, a lot of American couples started to take an interest in the 'electric body massagers' which were routinely advertised in women's magazines as being 'Great For Those Tired Muscles' or 'The Drug-Free Alternative If You've Got Rheumatism'.

Sales of the electric massagers started booming, and it soon became apparent that the explosion in sales was *not* due to a sudden outbreak of arthritis among US women! No, people were using the 'rheumatism aids' as a way of achieving orgasm.

I remember that in Britain I mentioned this trend in my column in *SHE* magazine. Soon afterwards, I received discreet thanks (but, alas, no money!) from one of the UK's biggest electrical retailers. They'd been amazed to find that their sales to British women had rocketed.

Not long after this, a tidal wave of purpose-designed vibrators started flooding into Western countries. Nearly all were made in the East, and the great majority were penis-shaped – which was actually not what many women wanted. Some were mains-powered – though this became less common as battery-powered devices became more popular.

By the mid-1970s, most vibrators were either white, ribbed, pointed, hard, cock-imitating devices (popular with males, but not with females), or else rather strange-looking black or black-and-gold cylinders which went under the forbidding name of 'Non-Doctor'.

They were not well-designed for stimulating the clitoris, so perhaps it's not surprising that women didn't go out and buy them in their droves!

Since then, vibrators have become far more widely accepted. It is claimed that 40,000 a month are bought by British couples, although that figure is very hard to verify.

One very good thing is that they've changed greatly in shape, to meet feminine requirements; many different varieties are now available. The newer, more colourful 'jelly-feel' vibrators are often much appreciated by women, as are the ergonomically-designed ones designed mainly for external use.

So how can they be used to enhance the enjoyment of sexual intercourse?

Well, although men still often think that a vibrator *must* be placed inside the vagina, the fact is that their main value is as a stimulator of the clitoris, and adjoining area. Employed as an adjunct to intercourse, they will give the woman considerably increased pleasure, and will often help her to reach climax after climax during sex.

Let's look at some examples:

THE BUTTERFLY VIBRATOR

Often known as 'Venus Butterfly' or 'Joni's Butterfly,' this is a simple device which straps on, so that it lies immediately in front of a girl's pubes.

You switch it on – and it buzzes away merrily in front of her clitoris. The guy can then penetrate her – most conveniently in a rear-entry position (*fig 43*).

fig 43

THE LIPSTICK VIBRATOR

This is a neat little device, which any woman may carry in her handbag without embarrassment. As you observe, she can easily use it during intercourse to give her clitoris a most agreeable buzz (*fig 44*).

fig 44

THE 'STANDARD' (PENILE-SHAPED) VIBRATOR

Generally, either the man or the woman places this on the clitoris (or just nearby) during intercourse.

Because these things are generally quite bulky, it's easier to use them in positions in which your tummies aren't pressed together – such as rear-entry, *cuissade* or *flanquette*. However, *smaller* vibrators are available (see above).

TONGUEJOY

A tiny vibrator which either the man or the woman can wear on the tip of a finger, which is then applied to the clitoris. It can also be worn on the man's cock, which transforms it into a 'flesh vibrator'! (As the name suggests, it can even be attached to the tongue.)

THE EROS-CTD

This is the first sex aid to have been approved by America's powerful Food & Drug Administration (FDA) – for the treatment of female sexual dysfunction. In fact, it is quite good fun for *any* open-minded woman, even if she has no dysfunction! It has recently gone on the market in the UK. Basically, it's a small suction device, which is placed over the clitoris. The idea is to increase clitoral blood flow – and therefore arousal. I recommend using it with a small vibrator on top of it. It is quite easy to have intercourse while you're employing it – particularly if the man is *behind* the woman. In Britain, the Eros-CTD is still very expensive (around £180-200), but it is quite easy to find other 'suction' sex aids which do a very similar job — and have a vibrator attached as well – for instance, the well-known Clit Seducer.

THE ANGEL'S EGG

This is small and egg-shaped (no surprises there, then…). It's connected to its battery pack by a wire. You can either put it over the woman's clitoris during intercourse, or else place it inside. The latter technique will only be comfortable if the man's penis is relatively small for the size of her vagina.

GEISHA BALLS

These famous Japanese balls are also useful if there is some disparity between the size of the penis and the size of the vagina. Just pop them inside before intercourse, and they will produce a pleasant feeling of bulk, which the woman would not have otherwise experienced.

This brings us to the 'Internal Vibrator Technique'. I developed it some years ago, as a way of helping women whose vaginas had become too wide or too loose, as a result of childbirth. This, by the way, is an extremely common, but rarely recognised, problem. Most mums who have had more than two children do feel that their vaginas are a little broader than they would like. This condition can be helped by pelvic

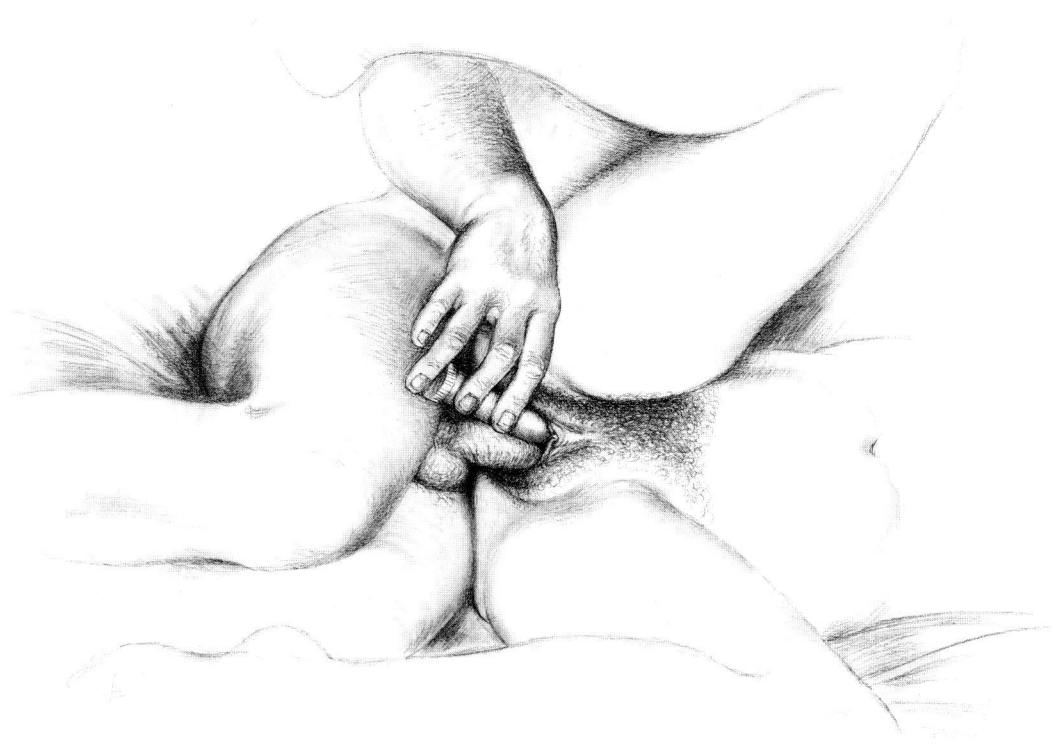

fig 45

exercises – or, if necessary, by having a 'tightening-up' operation.

(I must stress that tightening-up ops are not guaranteed to cure the problem – but they usually do help a lot. There are numerous possible surgical procedures, but the commonest one – which gynaecologists call a 'repair' or a 'colporrhaphy' – is carried out through the vulva. A diamond-shaped area of tissue is removed from the front wall of the vagina, and then the edges of the diamond are 'darned' together.)

But a useful temporary solution is this. The woman simply places a small (repeat *small*) vibrator in her vagina – alongside her partner's penis. Switch on, and enjoy both the vibrations and the comfortable feeling of bulk (*fig 45*).

For completeness, I should add that there are some vibrators which can be used on the *male* during sexual intercourse. These give considerable pleasure, and can often help with erection difficulties.

Among the ones I would recommend are:

THE PENISATOR

An amusing little buzzing device which can be fitted round the base of the man's cock, before he puts it inside the woman. A similar male vibrator for use during intercourse is the amusingly-named Sorbet Delight Cock Ring Set.

THE HANDSTRAP VIBRATOR

This is actually strapped to the woman's hand and she simply applies her fingers to the base of the man's organ during intercourse. Very jolly!

THE MICRO FINGER TICKLER

A high-powered massager which the woman puts on her finger; she then applies her fingertip to the base of the man's penis as he 'does' her...

MASSAGERS AND PROBES

All sorts of sophisticated massagers and probes can be used during sexual intercourse, and the range of them has expanded greatly during the last couple of years. Here are some examples:

THE VIELLE (*fig 46*)

Invented only recently, and released in the UK early in 2003, this is a little massager that the man wears on the tip of his finger, so that he can rub the clitoris more efficiently. The guy is wearing it on the

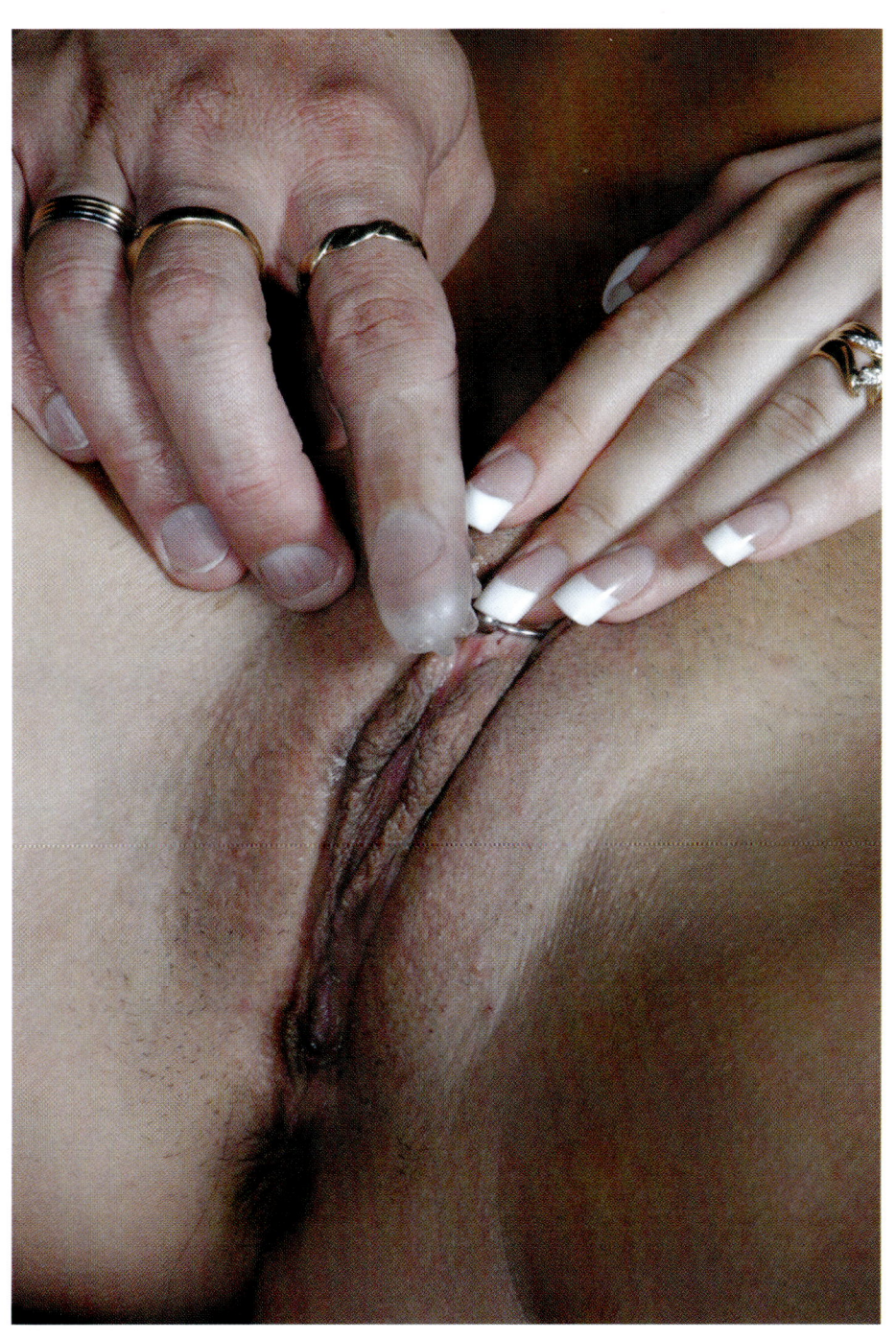

fig 46

SEXPERFECT

tip of his index finger while his stimulates his lover's clit – and can have intercourse with her from the rear. It's also perfectly possible for the woman to use it for self-stimulation during intercourse.

THE MASSAGE WAND (*fig 47*)

While this cunningly-designed 'girl's toy' is mainly designed for love play or self-stimulation, skilled lovers can also use it during sexual intercourse – particularly if the woman's vagina is roomy. If the man is behind the woman, he may even be able to reach her G-spot with it. (If you achieve this, I will personally send you a signed certificate…)

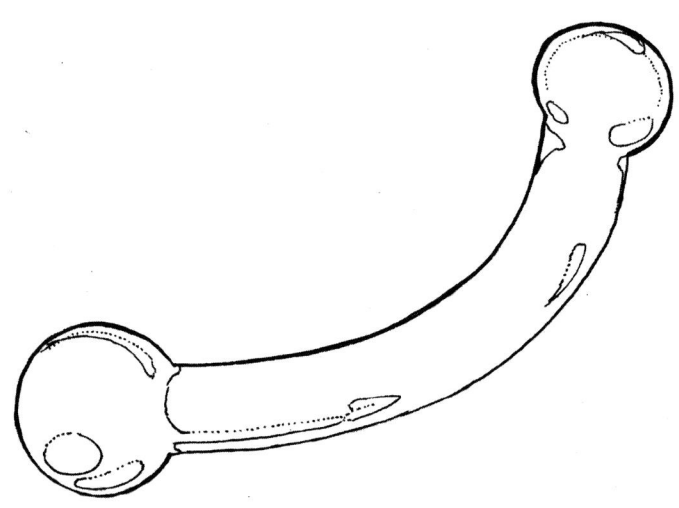

fig 47

THE GRADUATE PROBE (*fig 48*)

Again, this can be inserted alongside the penis – particularly if the bloke's cock is fairly small and the girl's pussy is on the broad side. Experts recommend whipping it out, just at the moment of female orgasm, so as to intensify her pleasure.

Note: Massagers and similar devices for anal sex-play are dealt with in Chapter Eight.

fig 48

THINGS TO WEAR ON THE PENIS

Sex aids are worn on the penis for two purposes: firstly, to give added stimulus to the woman's genitals; secondly, to give the man's cock added firmness and support – a matter of some importance if he tends to lose his erection.

The oldest such device is probably the 'Goat's Eye' – a ring of 'eyelashes' which fits round the penis, just below the head. The idea is that the lashes tickle the inside of the girl's vagina. I don't *think* that this sex aid was made from *real* goats' eyelashes…

One drawback with that invention – and with most other ring-like devices – is that they *may come off the cock during intercourse, and get lost inside the vagina.*

That isn't the end of the world, since most couples can manage to fish the ring out again. But if you can't find it, this means a visit to the gynaecologist – or the Accident & Emergency Department.

Nonetheless, there are quite a few 'worn on the penis' devices which I would recommend to any loving couple who are keen to experiment. They include:

THE CLITORAL STIMULATOR (*fig 49*)
This is a ring-like device, worn round the base of the penis. As you can see, it has a bumpy projection on top – and this rubs against the woman's clitoris during intercourse.

fig 49 (a) – (c)

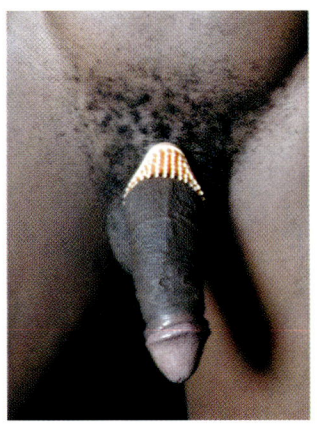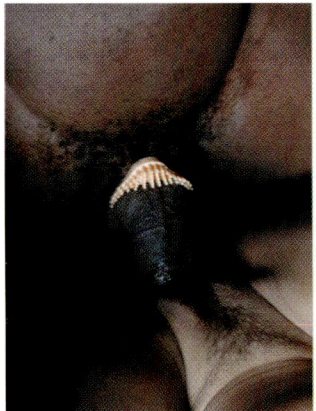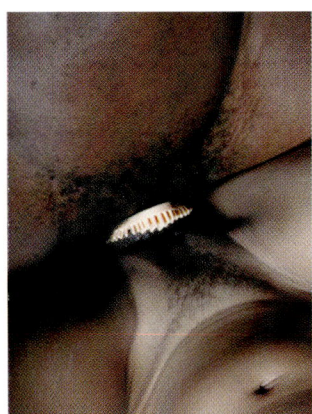

THE COCK RING (*fig 50*)
This stretchy little device fits round and (to some extent) supports the shaft of the penis. The bumps on it give some stimulus to the girl's labia.

THE BLAKOE ENERGISING RING

This traditional British sex aid was invented over 30 years ago. It's a thick, black ring that goes round the base of the penis *and* the testicles; it has small metal plates on it, which are supposed to generate a small electrical current.

It gives firmness to the shaft, and a certain amount of stimulation to the female's vulva. But generations of British males have used it because of its alleged value in combating impotence. Certainly, it gives a lot of men more confidence in bed.

THE CYBERSLEEVE AND MONROE'S LIPS

Sleevelike penile stimulators that 'pulse' up and down your shaft. However, they give you so much bulk that you may actually find it difficult to get inside your partner – unless her vaginal orifice is unusually wide.

CASE STUDY

Prudence worked in the Diplomatic Service. She had had a number of lovers before she met the man of her dreams, and married him.

Unfortunately, she was completely unable to reach orgasm – either during intercourse or during love play. Her new husband tried to help her, but simply could not 'bring her off.' This was a source of much distress to both of them.

Eventually, Prudence got hold of one of the famous videos of Betty Dodson, the celebrated American 'sexpert' who has taught so many women to reach orgasm. Betty takes groups of women and – with the aid of vibrators – shows them how they can come again and again. Prudence and her husband settled down one night and watched the videotape together. Both of them became pretty aroused at the sight of all those feisty, determined American females, each of them learning how to climax.

Next day, Prudence went out and bought herself a vibrator. Then she and her man watched the video again, while she followed the redoubtable Betty's instructions.

Half-way through, she climaxed for the first time in her life.

Her husband then took the vibrator from her shaking hands, and began to use it on her. Five minutes later, she climaxed for the second time in her life. From then on, it was onwards and upwards for this happy couple. They soon learned how to use the clever little device during intercourse, so that Prudence was able to come whenever she wanted to – and with her man inside her.

PENIS ENHANCEMENT RINGS

Cheerfully coloured rings which fit round the base of the penis.

STRETCHY SILICONE PENIS EXTENSIONS

These fit over the end of the penis, and are said to give you an extra two and a quarter inches (6 cms). They also glow in the dark, if that's what you fancy.

MUMFORD'S PENIS RINGS

Designed for use with the Owen Mumford Vacuum Pump, but can be used on their own to restrict the amount of blood flowing out of the penis – and so promote the erection.

There are many different sex aids that can enhance your lovemaking and these are just a few of them. More are constantly coming onto the market, and if you like the look of some new device that you see in a mail-order brochure, it may well be worth trying it.

fig 50

exotic positions which alter the angle of penetration

In Chapter Two, we looked at how some simple alterations of sexual position make it possible to change the angle at which the penis enters the vagina – thus producing new and interesting sensations for both parties.

Now in this chapter, we're going to look at some slightly less well-known positions, and at how they can create unusual and agreeable feelings in the sex organs. Most of them are illustrated by helpful photographs. Let's begin:

THE FLORENCE POSITION (*fig 51*)

There seems to be a general view that this position may have been invented in the fair city of Florence, perhaps by one of the dark-eyed beauties who used to go cruisin' on that amusin' Ponte Vecchio…

Anyway, it's a jolly good *postura*, and an excellent feature of it is that it's a great help to the many men who have slight uncertainties about their erections.

Why? Because it brings the woman's hand into play, that's why. And what she does with her skilled hand can be of enormous value in keep the man's penis stiff.

What happens is that the man lies flat on his back, with his organ pointing skywards. The *signorina* then mounts him while on her knees and facing him.

But the big trick is this. She puts her hand *behind* her back, grasps his shaft – and stimulates it vigorously while she bounces merrily up and down on top of him.

Obviously, what she does with her hand can give the man some really nice sensations. And, by moving his penis around to various angles, she can alter the sensations that *she* feels too. Furthermore,

fig 51
(a) – (d)

and most importantly, her fingers can ensure that he remains erect.

Incidentally, the late (and much missed) sexpert Dr Alex Comfort used to say that to get the very best out of this position, the woman should pull the guy's penile skin – including his foreskin – as far *downwards* as possible, releasing it only at the moment of orgasm.

THE STRAUSS POSITION (*fig 52*)

There are those who claim that this one was invented by Richard Strauss while composing his erotic and sensuous 'bedroom suite' *Symphonia Domestica*.

Be that as it may, the position does give the woman unique and pleasing pressures on the side wall, of her vagina... and it's pretty *gemütlich* for the bloke too.

How do you get into it? This needs time – and care.

Ladies: begin by lying the man flat on his back. Then make sure you give him a good erection. Next, kneel astride him, facing away from him – and lower yourself onto him.

Once he's firmly inside you, turn your entire body through 90 degrees till you're facing sideways, and then lean forward until you're *lying across him, face downwards*. You'll find that getting one of your legs straight is a bit tricky, but it can be done! So you finish up at right-angles to your feller – just like the young woman in the picture. Enjoy!

The chief defect of this position is that the guy has practically no access to your clitoris. However, he does have excellent access to your bottom, if you fancy that type of thing. (And if you *do*, see Chapter Eight.)

fig 52
(a) – (c)

THE NARBONNE POSITION (*fig 53*)

This is a good position for lovers who want to try something that is comfortable and romantic – but which also gives a slightly unusual angle of entry into the vagina.

 As you can see, the woman sits on the edge of a couch or bed, with her knees bent and legs raised. The man now kneels on the

fig 53

floor in front of her, preferably on a comfortable cushion.

She can then draw him in quite deeply, and once he's inside she can – if she wishes – cross her legs behind him and draw him in even further with her thighs.

Warning: the Narbonne position is not ideal for gentlemen who have rheumaticky knees. But if you do have a spot of arthritis, and still want to try it, I would strongly recommend a couple of aspirin or a Voltarol taken 45 minutes beforehand. Good luck!

THE BRISTOL POSITION (*fig 54*)

An entertaining position, in which the woman can achieve a constantly changing series of vaginal sensations as she *rotates* herself on her man's erect staff. Women can proceed as follows: lie your man flat on his back. Stand astride him, facing towards him. Then lower yourself gently onto him until you can pop him inside, while sitting on him.

fig 54

As you can see from the picture, your thighs are spread wide. This gives your man an excellent opportunity for stimulating your clitoris –

CASE STUDY

Dilys worked in the world of high finance. She was an English Rose – strictly brought up, and knowing little of sexual matters.

Unfortunately, she married a chap – also a financial wizard, incidentally – who was pretty uptight and who had had few sexual experiences. He never made love except in any other position than the 'good old missionary.' Indeed, he thought that to do so in any other position was rather rude...

Not altogether surprisingly, Dilys was less than happy with her love-life. It gave her little satisfaction. But she put up with it for ten years – which was when she decided to divorce her husband. He did not contest the case, especially as he had his eye on another woman – who he felt would be less 'demanding' in bed.

After the divorce, Dilys began to look around – and even tried speed-dating! That was where she met a distinguished-looking gynaecologist. She liked the idea of 'trying him out' because she felt that at least this man would know about women's bodies...

Well, he did. On their first date, he took her to bed and astonished her by 'bringing her off' several times with his tongue. Then, to her delight, he showed her half-a-dozen different intercourse positions – most of which she'd never even heard of.

Their relationship continues happily to this day. And so far, he's taken her more than 20 different ways. What a contrast with her miserable, love-starved marriage!

which is what our male model is doing – cunningly employing his left thumb for the purpose.

Now comes the really unusual thing about the Bristol position. Helped by the man, the woman gently turns herself through a full circle.

Yes, she goes through 360 degrees – first facing sidewards, then facing away from her partner, and so on till eventually she is facing him again. In nautical parlance, this is known as 'Boxing The Compass'.

THE SEVILLE POSITION
(*fig 55*)

This exotic position is so called because it was invented at the Hotel Alfonso XIII – the finest and most luxurious hostelry in the famous and exciting city where Carmen and the Barber both enjoyed bedtime frolics (in separate operas, of course). Why is it good? Because the *señor* can actually see the *señorita's* pubic area, and so can position his fingers very accurately. That's why this position rarely fails.

To get into the Seville proceed as follows. The gent should be on the bed, on his back. He should be lying down one *side* of the bed – not in the middle.

The woman then sits herself comfortably down on him, facing sideways, and with her legs dangling over the edge. Once she is comfortable with him inside her, she can guide his hand to her clit, to her breasts or to wherever else she wants.

Will they both come in this position? I certainly hope so! More about climaxing in the next chapter…

fig 55

coming inside... and outside

I suppose it's fair to say that the main objective of sexual intercourse is to climax – biologically speaking, anyway. In terms of the survival of humanity, orgasm (or at any rate, *male* orgasm), is clearly the point of the whole thing.

My research partner and I have been conducting an ongoing survey on the subject of orgasm over the last nine years, and we have carried out a study of male and female orgasm, and have even interviewed transexuals about how the 'Big O' felt before and after the op (different!). There are similarities between male and female orgasm, in that they both involve intense pleasure, and are typified by contractions occurring every 0.8 seconds. However, female orgasm is in general a rather more emotional (even spiritual) experience.

But as we'll see in a moment, for a lot of people coming isn't really the principal objective. This is particularly true of women – many of whom value the closeness and intimacy of intercourse more than the actual climax.

Also, many older men eventually find that reaching orgasm isn't quite as easy as it once was. So they too may start to appreciate an enjoyable session of intercourse as *an objective in itself*.

I do think that it's important not to regard climaxing as the 'be-all and end-all' of sexual intercourse. But of course, it's a wonderful feeling when you come! So this chapter will sum up the major facts about orgasm during coitus.

Let's begin with *female* climaxes.

FEMALE ORGASM
FIRST ORGASM

At the moment, the commonest age of first orgasm among British women is 19. This is quite startling when you look at the statistic in the next paragraph.

FIRST INTERCOURSE

In Britain, the average age of first intercourse is now down to just below 17 (which *does* seem incredibly young!). But the point to note is that this is roughly *two years* before the average age of first orgasm.

Now, vast numbers of people – especially younger people – think that if a girl has intercourse, she should immediately be able to climax. These figures make clear that in fact orgasm is quite uncommon during the early years of intercourse.

HOW DO MOST WOMEN REACH ORGASM?

Many men and women still have the mistaken idea that most female orgasms are obtained through intercourse – without clitoral stimulation. This just isn't true. Our figures show that only about 13% of orgasms are obtained through intercourse alone.

In contrast, 87% of female climaxes are obtained through some direct form of stimulation of the clitoris – either during intercourse, or during love-play alone.

ARE ORGASMS DURING INTERCOURSE BETTER THAN OTHER ONES?

If you're a man, you probably think that a woman would greatly prefer an orgasm that occurs during intercourse to any other type.

In fact, our figures don't back that up.

We have been quite surprised to find that most British women (60%) say that they prefer the orgasms that they get through sex-play to the ones they get during sexual intercourse!

This probably parallels the common *male* experience that a climax induced by the hand can be more intense than one which occurs in the vagina.

CAN WOMEN CLIMAX AT WILL – AS MOST MEN CAN?

Emphatically – no! About two-thirds of all women say that they can't simply climax whenever they want to. Furthermore, about half of all females say that they're *worried* by the fact that they 'take too long in coming' or 'can't come during intercourse'.

Male readers should, of course, bear these facts in mind and try to be helpful and understanding when having intercourse with a partner who isn't quick to reach climax.

Common (but potentially hurtful) remarks like, 'Haven't you come yet, love?' should be avoided!

SIMULTANEOUS ORGASMS DURING INTERCOURSE

One of the big myths about female orgasm is that it's supposed to take place at exactly the same moment as the male's orgasm. This idea has been reinforced by the countless romantic or erotic stories which so many women (and men) have read in which the hero and the heroine invariably come together in a blaze of glory!

The truth is that simultaneous orgasm isn't really all that common. Two skilled lovers who know each other's bodies very well *can* often achieve it. But on the majority of occasions, it just doesn't happen.

Indeed, our figures show that only one woman in 50 says that she 'always' comes at the same moment as her man. About 60% say that it 'sometimes' happens.

And for about a fifth of all couples, orgasm is 'never' simultaneous.

Actually, simultaneous climaxes give you a delightful shared experience. If you want to achieve them, later in this chapter I'll tell you how…

DO WOMEN SQUIRT OUT A JET OF FLUID WHEN THEY COME DURING INTERCOURSE?

Many men have this idea – which they've generally obtained from porn novels. ('As His Majesty the King reached his royal climax inside the fair Arethusa, he realised with satisfaction that she was releasing the flood of feminine dew which indicated that she too had reached the very topmost peak of joy…')

However, the notion of female ejaculation is largely, but not entirely, a myth – a myth that has been passed down through the centuries since it was first popularised in books like John Cleland's 18th-century classic, *Fanny Hill*.

I say that it is not entirely a myth because of the fact that, since the 1970s, it has been clear that there is a small group of women who really do squirt out something when they come.

This is not common. During all of Masters' and Johnson's famous researches on hundreds of American women who obligingly climaxed in the laboratory in front of the two scientists' eyes, they did not find one subject who 'squirted'. But men who have had many mistresses will often say, 'Yes – there was *one* who drenched my sheets…'

Somewhere around 1977, I began to get a large number of letters from women who were deeply distressed by the fact that (as they saw it) they 'wet the bed' at the moment of orgasm. Initially – like most doctors – I thought that they must have just been passing urine.

However, research by Whipple *et al* seems to have established without much doubt that for some females, it is *normal* to pass a quantity of fluid when they come. It is claimed that this fluid is similar to the liquid produced by the male's prostate gland, and that it originates in the region of the G-spot.

Therefore a woman who habitually 'squirts' during sexual intercourse shouldn't feel bad about it. Far from it! Indeed, women should remember that many male partners will think that this is absolutely *great*! A man tends to assume that if you produce a jet of fluid, then that shows what a great lover he is… However, you will need to ensure that you always have sex on top of a thick towel.

MALE ORGASM

Our ongoing survey proves – if proof were needed – that orgasm is a very different experience in males.

Here are the results to date:

FIRST ORGASM

In the average British male, this occurs at 13. But we have found a range varying from 10 (good heavens!) to 17.

AGE OF FIRST INTERCOURSE

Rather alarmingly, this age has kept decreasing in recent years. We agree with other surveys that it is now hovering around the mark of 16 years. I say that that's alarming because many lads of this age have absolutely no idea about contraception – or about the risks of sexually transmitted diseases. And let's be blunt: the less education a boy has, the more likely he is to get himself into trouble through early sex. So it's the least well educated who find themselves having to cope with being teenage dads.

WAS THE FIRST ACT OF INTERCOURSE RUSHED?

Almost 50% of male respondents replied 'Yes' to this question. That is a figure of some importance, since 'rushed first intercourse' has often been cited as a cause of Premature Ejaculation.

HOW COMMON IS PREMATURE EJACULATION?

Premature Ejaculation ('PE' or 'Coming too soon') really messes up sexual intercourse for a lot of men – and their partners. But how common is it?

That depends on how you define the word 'premature'. But in our survey, a staggering 11% of men told us, 'I always come too soon.' Furthermore, another 60% say that they 'sometimes' climax too early – and therefore have to terminate intercourse sooner than they meant to.

Did we find any correlation between *rushed* first intercourse and PE? *In other words, is it true that if losing your virginity was an over-*

hasty experience, that can 'condition' you to coming too soon for the rest of your life?

Well, there does seem to be at least some relationship between rushed first coitus and PE. We find that 'early rushers' *are* more likely to be premature ejaculators than other guys. The figures are:

- 18% of those who experienced a rushed first intercourse now have PE;
- Only 6% of those who didn't experience a rushed first intercourse have PE.

The full causes of Premature Ejaculation remain unclear. But rushed loss of virginity is almost certainly one of them.

Please note that if PE is spoiling *your* enjoyment of intercourse, it can be treated these days – and usually cured. There are more details on this in our Epilogue.

SO HOW LONG DOES INTERCOURSE LAST?

We asked the men whom we surveyed to tell us 'How long does intercourse usually last for you?'

The average of their replies was 22 minutes – which sounds pretty good. However, the women to whom we posed the same question gave quite different answers. On average, they reckoned that intercourse lasted only eight or nine minutes!

Quite a disparity there. And in our clinical practice, we do find again and again that males think that they've spent adequate time on intercourse before they climax – while females complain that 'it was all over far too quickly.'

Interestingly, about a fifth of all men do honestly admit that for them, intercourse generally lasts less than *five minutes*. I'm afraid that this is not nearly enough for today's sexually liberated women.

DO MEN PREFER ORGASMS FROM SEX PLAY – OR ORGASMS FROM INTERCOURSE?

As already mentioned, a striking finding of our survey is that many women do prefer the orgasmic sensations they achieve through sex-play to the ones they experience when coming during intercourse.

In striking contrast, the great majority of males (75% of them, in fact) prefer the orgasms of intercourse to the ones of foreplay. This is despite the fact that many men frankly admit that 'finger pressure' can produce the most intense penile sensations. As the chap who wrote a parody of the song *Funiculi, Funicula* put it:

Sexual intercourse, of course,
Is absolutely grand.
But for personal satisfaction –
I prefer the hand.

So why do men generally prefer to reach orgasm through intercourse? Almost certainly, it's because the human male is biologically programmed to want – more than anything else in the world – to *discharge his semen inside a woman.*

This is without doubt one of the main reasons why the human race is still surviving on this planet!

CLIMAXING INSIDE – OR OUT?

It's a fact that generally speaking, both men *and* women tend to prefer the man to 'finish' (i.e. come) as deep inside the vagina as possible.

But these days, some couples do appear to like trying the variation of having the male pull out at the last minute and climax over the woman's body – usually over her pubes, which is obviously the most accessible part (*fig 56*).

Some men and women like to have the gentleman do it over the girl's breasts – just as the famous American action painter, Jackson Pollock, used to 'splatter' his canvasses. But the man has to move pretty swiftly to achieve this feat – unless, of course, he's the type of younger guy who can 'shoot' about four feet from his position between his partner's thighs!

DO MEN CLAIM THAT THEY AND THEIR PARTNERS HAVE SIMULTANEOUS CLIMAXES?

As you may have read in the first half of this chapter, women say that simultaneous orgasm isn't really that common.

And men replied in much the same way: only about 2% of them claim that they 'always' reach orgasm at the same instant as their partners. But about six out of 10 guys say that they 'sometimes' achieve it.

HOW TO REACH SIMULTANEOUS ORGASM

Simultaneous orgasm is definitely not essential – but it is very agreeable. If you really want to achieve it regularly, this is what guys should do:

fig 56

CASE STUDY

Alexander had been married twice. His first wife, Jessie, was quite a passionate lady, and usually enjoyed a tumble on the bed with him.

But, like a substantial minority of wives, she had never really got round to accepting the idea of male 'cum'.

When Alexander climaxed inside her, she made no secret of the fact that she detested the feeling of 'all that stuff dripping out of me for hours.' She thought that semen was 'disgusting', and said that it reminded her of 'undercooked fried egg'.

This didn't really do a lot for Alexander's self-esteem.

Eventually they divorced, and Alexander found and married a new girl, called Catriona. She was a redhead from the Isle of Skye, and her love-making was fiery.

In dramatic contrast to Jessie, she absolutely loved the idea of men coming, and producing lots of spunk. She regarded Alexander's 'cum' as a big tribute to her sexiness – and really wanted lots of it inside her. She actually liked the idea that it would drip out of her for the next few hours – she called it 'my wee erotic reminder'.

And on the few occasions when they agreed that Alexander would come over her body, she nearly went berserk! She delighted in massaging it into her breasts, and in rubbing it into her clitoris. Invariably, doing this made her climax once again.

Tell me now, dear readers: which of his wives was Alexander happier with?

- Have sex with a partner who can reach orgasm easily – indeed, preferably one who is multi-orgasmic

- Teach yourself all the techniques of sex play and clitoral stimulation – not just the ones in this book, but also the ones in our companion volume, *Sex Play*

- Talk to her about what you're trying to do – and find out the things that really turn her on

- Decide with her roughly how long she wants intercourse to last.

- If she's multi-orgasmic, get some idea of how many climaxes she'd like to have before you have yours!

- Tell yourself that you will *not* reach orgasm until she is absolutely ready; be very firm with yourself on this point!

- When you are almost ready to come, then make sure that you stimulate her clitoris in the way she likes best, and to the very best of your ability; if you do it right, then there's a good chance that you'll bring her off just at the moment that you start pumping…

If you both really want to do it, then you *can* achieve it – and 'come together'(*fig 57*). Good luck!

fig 57

adding anal play during intercourse

This book is actually about vaginal intercourse, not rectal intercourse. So much has already been written on this rich and fascinating way of making love that it should probably be treated as a different subject altogether. But there's no doubt that *vaginal* sexual intercourse can be made even more exciting by introducing a spot of *anal* play.

Indeed, I've known quite a few patients who found that *postillionage* (which is the Victorian term for stimulating the anus with your fingers) was just the thing to help them with slight difficulties like:

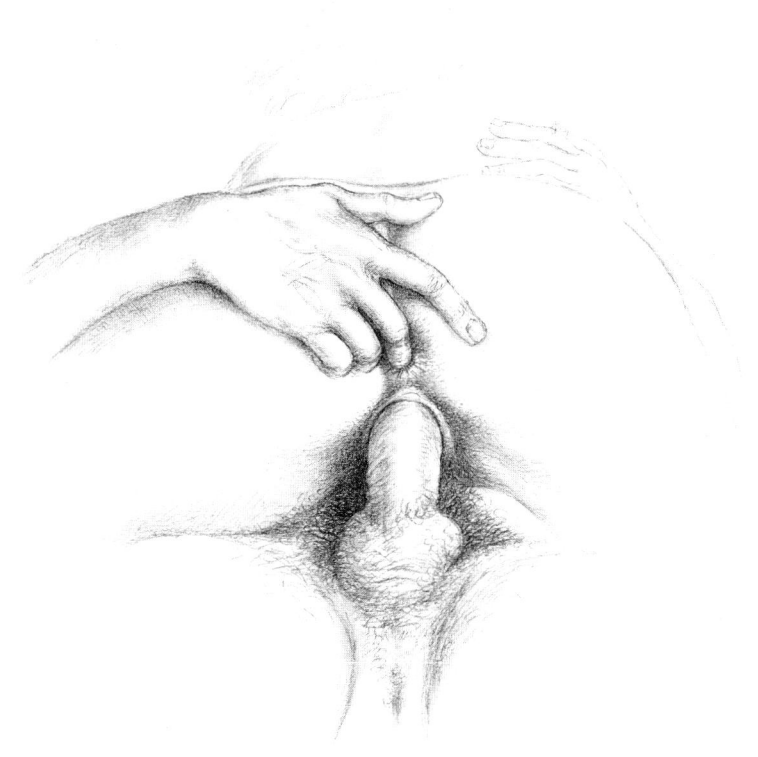

fig 58

- Poor erections
- Difficulty in reaching male orgasm
- Difficulty in reaching female orgasm

Obviously, a man can use his fingers to play with a woman's anus (*fig 58*) – or vice versa (*fig 59*). Either way, it can provide a dramatic sexual stimulus.

However, some people remain pretty doubtful about using anal stimulation. The main reasons for this are:

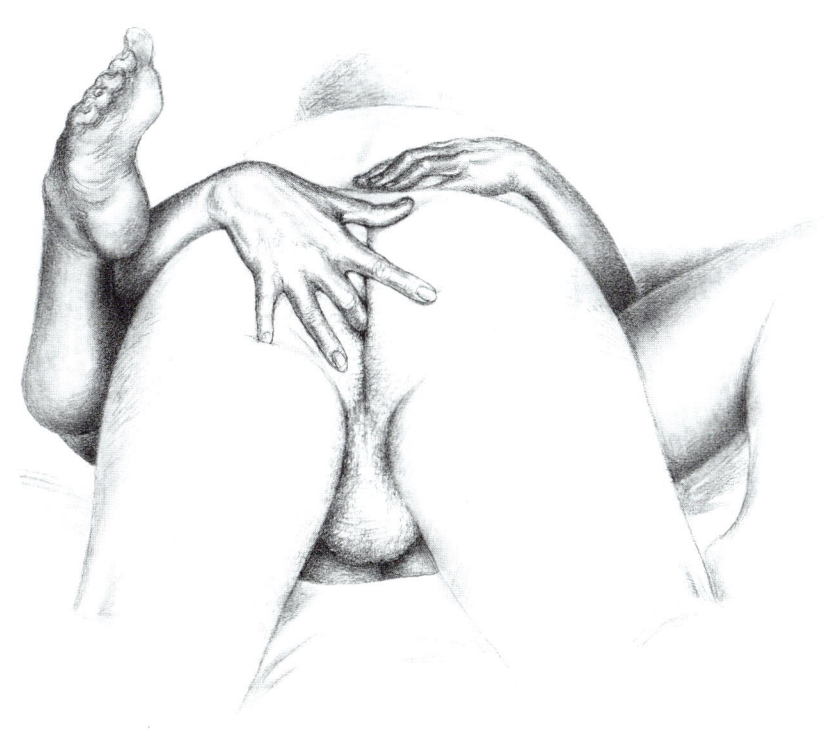

fig 59

• Hang-ups. Some men and women have appreciable hang-ups about the anal area – generally dating from early childhood and toilet training

• Worries about homosexuality. Some guys think that to show any interest in the rectal area indicates latent gayness – but this just isn't true

• Hygienic worries about the anus – see below (if you'll forgive the expression)

• Finally, quite a few people do sometimes have *sore* anuses! If you're having trouble with piles (or whatever), you may not feel very much like having anal fun…

But it's important to grasp the simple medical truth that the *derrière* is very, very rich in erotogenic (that is, sexually-linked) nerve endings. That's true not just of the buttocks, but also of the anal 'ring'.

Moralists who disapprove of the fact that the bottom is one of the major erotic areas of the body should address their complaints to the Designer – not to me.

HYGIENE

But there is a definite *caveat* where the bum is concerned. And it's to do with the question of hygiene.

I'm a doctor, so I would ask you to believe me when I tell you that the anus is *not* the cleanest area of the body. Quite unlike the penis or the vagina, it *does* tend to have germs *on* it, and *in* it.

These bowel germs can cause various infections – notably urinary tract problems in women (such as cystitis). More rarely, they could cause food poisoning (if they get into your grub) or hepatitis.

Therefore, if you want to go in for anal play, there are certain medical rules that I would strongly recommend to you:

- After you've finished touching your partner's anal area, wash your hands as soon as is practicable
- Having touched the anus with a finger, do not put that finger anywhere near the vagina – you could cause a vaginal discharge, or cystitis
- If someone is going to put a finger *inside* your bottom, it's wise to pop off to the loo first – and to make sure that your rectum is empty!

Now – on to the techniques which you and your partner can use during intercourse…

FINGER TECHNIQUES

I suggest that you use plenty of preliminary lubricant when employing these techniques. Unlike the vagina, the anus isn't a naturally self-lubricating organ! Put a good slurp of your chosen lubricant on your fingertip – and on your loved one's bottom.

FEMALE GIVING MALE ANAL STIMULATION

Girls will find this easiest in a face-to-face position; it's difficult in rear-entry ones. While you are having intercourse with your man, just slip your well-lubricated fingertip inside his bottom, and gently jiggle it around. It helps if you have long arms!

One word of caution: this sudden stimulation might just possibly fire him off into an orgasm before he – or you – are ready, so don't rush things.

There is also a highly sophisticated variation of this caress, in which the woman uses her fingertip during intercourse to stroke the man's prostate (*fig 60*). Exciting though this sounds, I have to tell you that it is impossible in most intercourse positions.

But it's quite easy if the couple adopt the posture called The Toy Boy – in which the man lies on top of the woman, but *at right angles to her*. This is exactly the reverse of the Strauss position shown in Chapter Six. The beauty of the Toy Boy position is that it gives the woman unrivalled access to the gentleman's bottom, to do with as she will.

MALE GIVING FEMALE ANAL STIMULATION

This method is usually quite easy for a man to do, because men tend to have relatively long arms. Men should take it very gently – because a woman's anal orifice is generally pretty small. It's usual to start with the index finger or little finger; if your lover gets to like this kind of thing, she may be willing to try the middle finger instead (*fig 61*).

When the two of you know each other's bodies well, and when she is used to anal stimulation, she may well let you slip your entire finger inside her while you are having intercourse with her. Passionate women say that this gives them very intense pelvic sensations – like being entered by two penises at once.

A refinement of this technique is for the man to have his index finger inside the girl's rectum, and his penis inside her vagina. He can in fact use his fingertip to stroke his own cock – through the thin partition that divides the vagina from the rectum. Interestingly, some exotically minded women find that idea very exciting (*fig 62*).

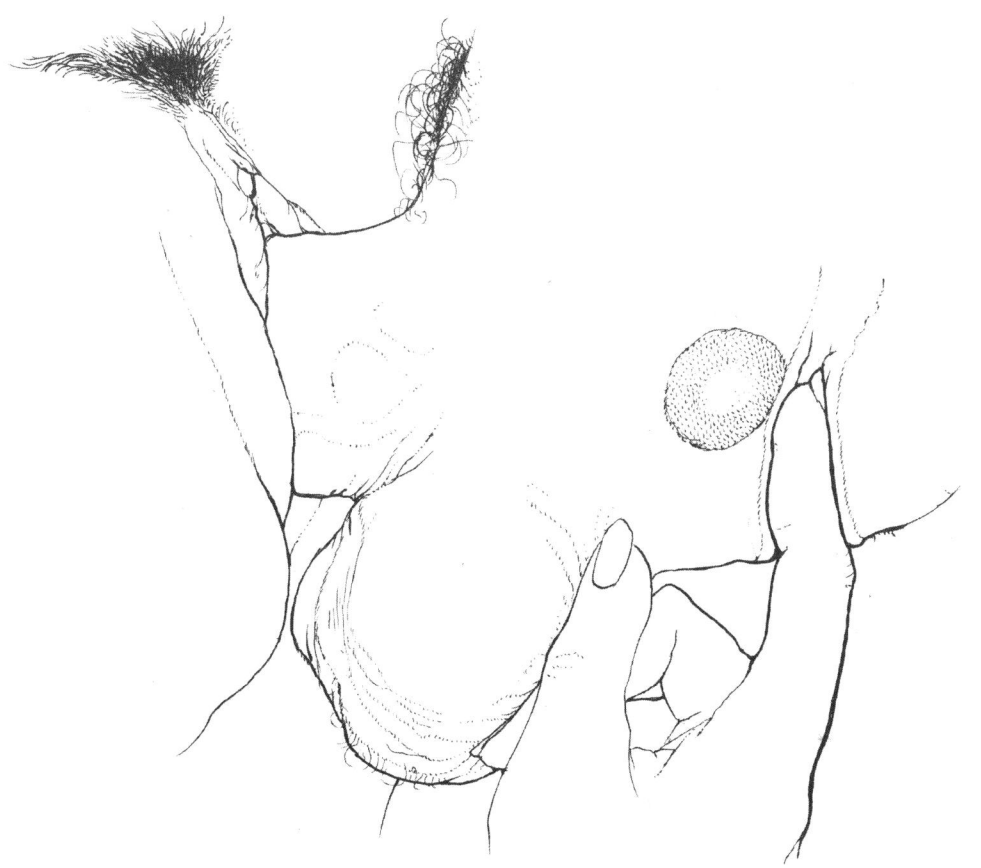

fig 60

SEX AID TECHNIQUES

In recent years, a lot of couples have found that sexual intercourse can be made even more fun by using rectal sex toys.

Three minor words of warning:

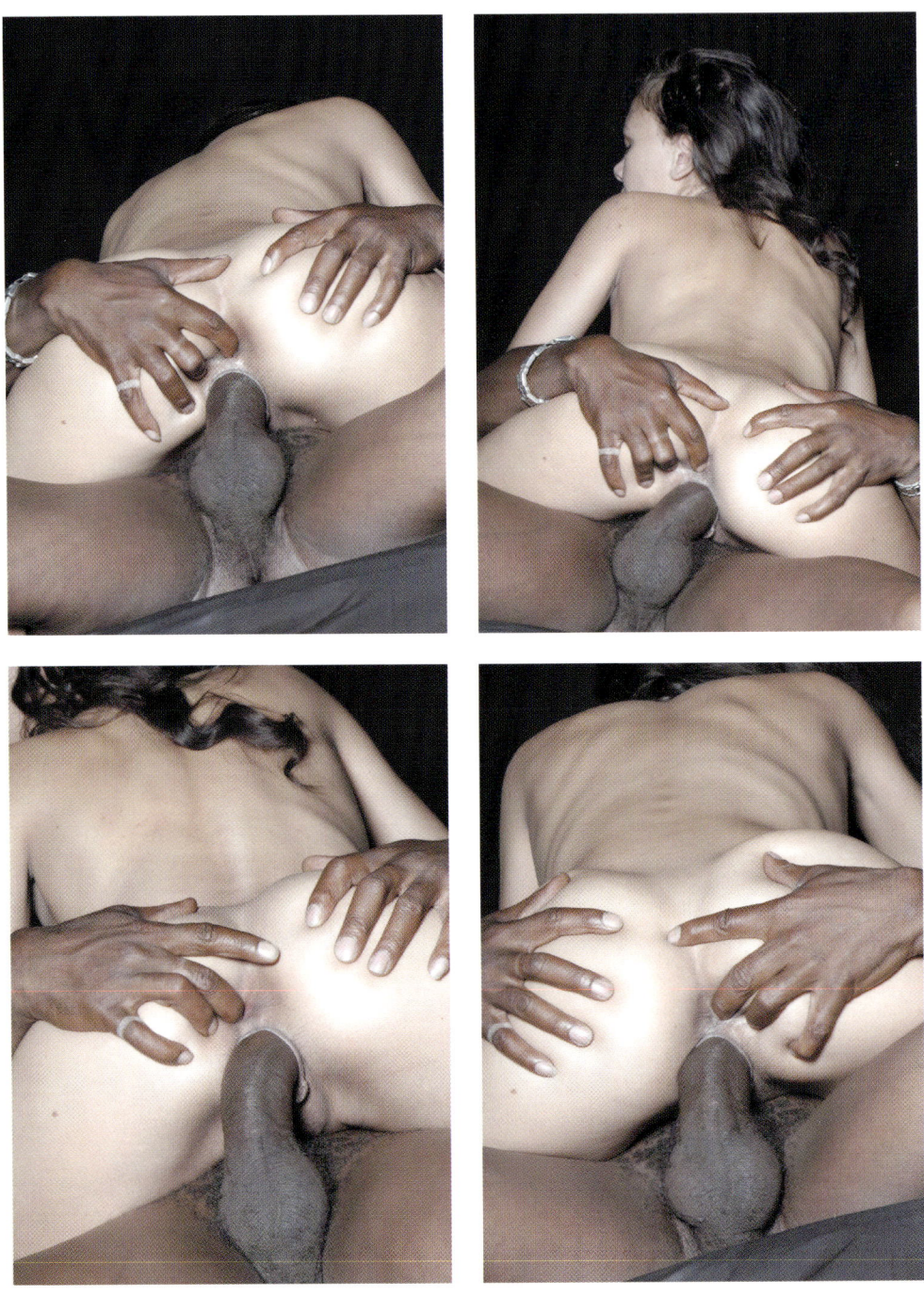

fig 61
(a) – (d)

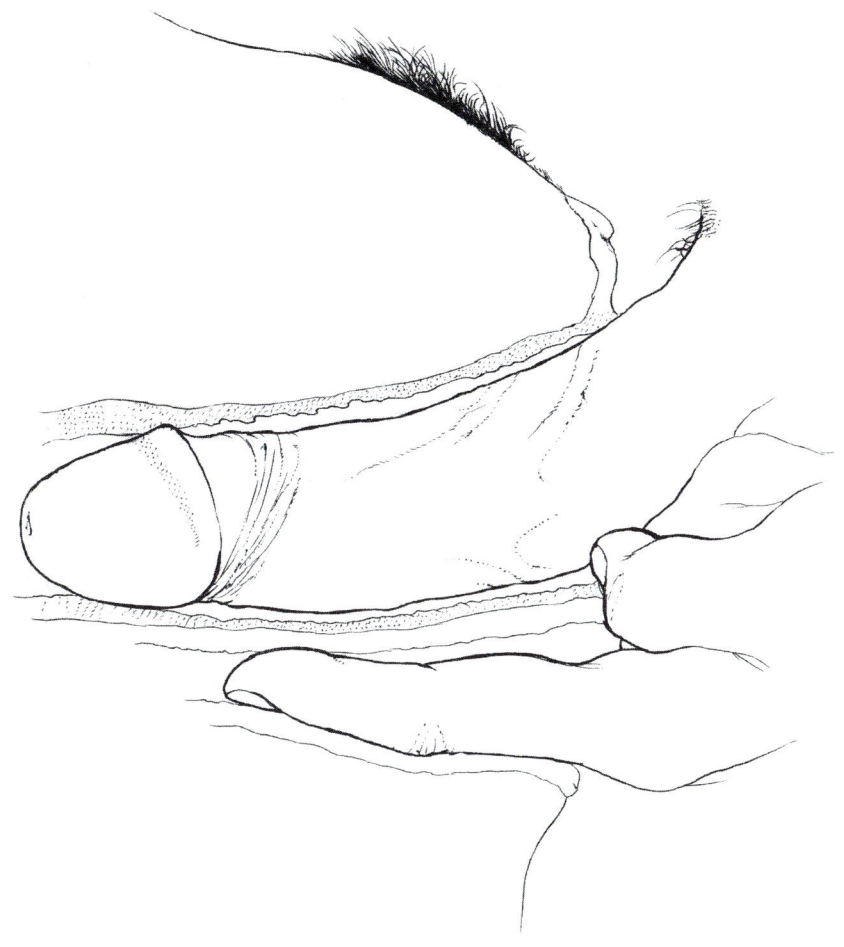

fig 62

- Take the same hygienic precautions as you would when using your fingers (see above)
- Because your partner's bottom is rather a long way away from you while you are having face-to-face intercourse, it can be a bit difficult for you to *control* a sex aid – so take care that you don't give your lover a nasty jab up the bum!
- Only use *purpose-designed* anal sex aids. Why? Because vaginal

vibrators and other aids are notorious for disappearing up people's bottoms – and not coming back

If a sex aid vanishes up your posterior, this will mean – at the very least – an embarrassing trip to hospital. That will probably be highly amusing for the doctors, but not for you. Incidentally, they will be on the look-out for the 'oscillating umbilicus sign' – which indicates that a vibrator is stuck somewhere in the region of the navel…

Fortunately, today's rectal sex aids are usually designed with a wide base or a flange which prevents them from vanishing into the dark interior. But still, *prenez garde* !

Now here are some of the things you can use on your lover's anus:

RECTAL VIBRATORS

These work extremely well during intercourse, though they can be quite difficult for women – with their slightly shorter arms – to put into men. Whether you're male or female, having one buzzing away in your bottom at the moment when you climax can be very pleasing indeed (*fig 63*).

THAI BEADS

Known by various names, these are little spherical devices that you generally whip out of your lover's rectum at the moment of her climax (*fig 64*). My patients tell me that they seem to work better on women than men.

Note: please only use beads sold by reputable suppliers, which are guaranteed by them not to break – or to disappear inside.

fig 63

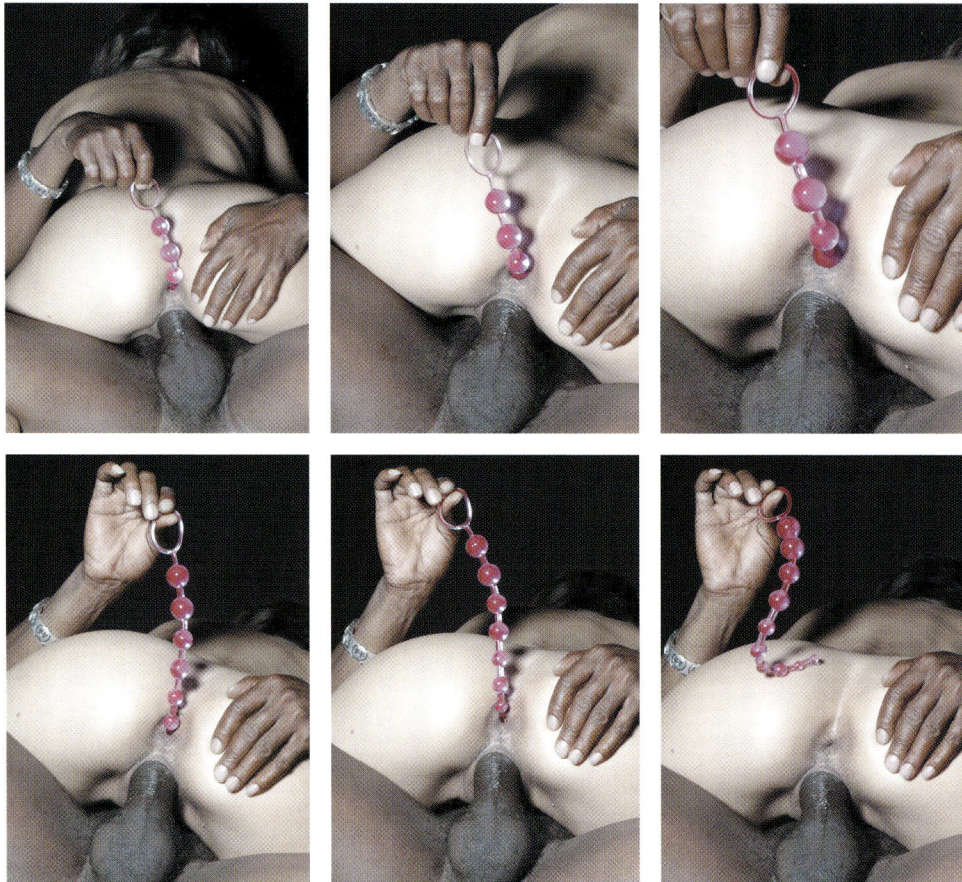

fig 64
(a) – (f)

SMALL DILDO

Many couples practise the game of putting a small dildo (artificial penis) into the girl's rectum and keeping it in there during intercourse. This gives her an agreeable feeling of fullness as well as the now popular fantasy of 'double penetration' – i.e. being penetrated by two lovers. (Again, please only employ a dildo that is designed for rectal use.)

BUTT PLUG

This is a fairly wide, conical-shaped device for putting into your lover's bottom. The point of the wide base is to make sure that it can't become 'lost property' (*fig 65*).

PADDLES, ETC.

For completeness, I should say that a lot of couples who enjoy a spot of bottom smacking do tend to go in for it during intercourse; here (*fig 66*) a game young woman is urging on her muscular lover with the aid of a ping-pong bat on his buttocks (although more custom-designed paddles are available!).

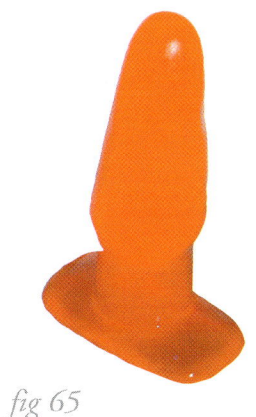

fig 65

CASE STUDY

Liam and Philomena were an Irish couple whom I saw some time ago. He was a poet, and she was a barrister.

They loved each other very much, and they said that in bed they had 'a great time – a great time.'

But – probably owing to Philomena's strict upbringing she had a bit of trouble in coming. She had never managed to do it during intercourse.

I gave them various love play tips, but whatever they tried she couldn't quite get there.

Then, one night, on a romantic holiday in Donegal, they came up with the solution…

Liam was making love to Philomena, and rubbing her clitoris with his right hand at the same time. He heard her say, 'Oh hell – I'm almost bloody there! I just need a little bit more…'

Without thinking, he dipped his forefinger in an Irish coffee which was sitting by the bed – and then touched her rear end with the fingertip. She immediately screamed out loud with delight – and came.

So that's how they do it now – though the Irish coffee definitely isn't essential…

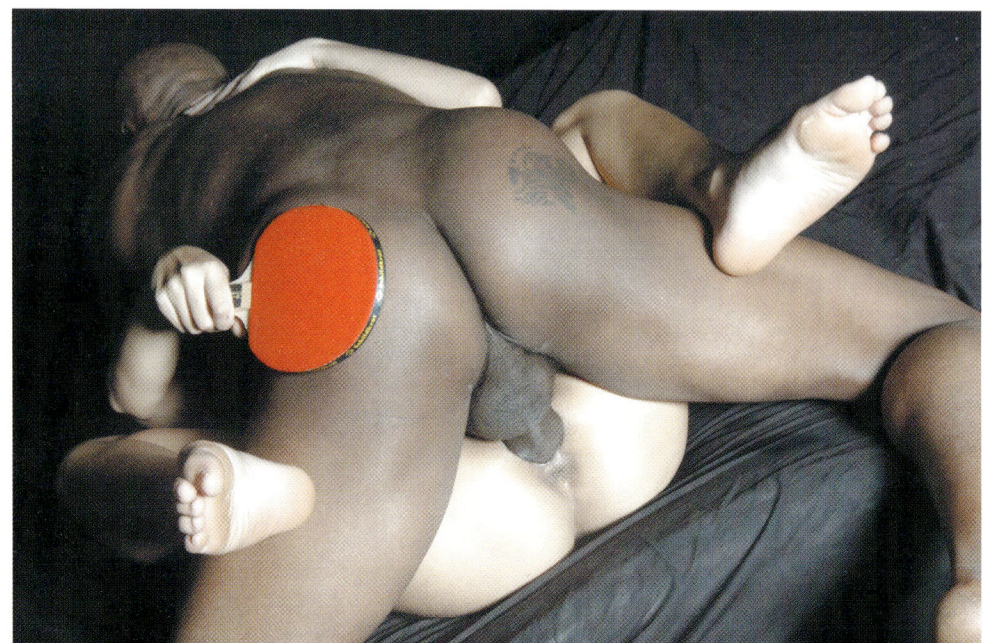

fig 65
(a) – (b)

fig 66 (d)

Epilogue

Sexual intercourse is a wonderful thing – and I hope this book has helped you to enjoy it even more than you did before.

But – as is the case with any human activity – problems can sometimes arise. The common difficulties which occur in connection with intercourse are:

- In men, problems with erection;
- Also in men, premature ejaculation;
- In both sexes, inability to come;
- In women, pain during sexual intercourse;
- Also in women, inability to enjoy intercourse.

Happily, all these problems can be successfully treated these days. If you or your partner suffers from one of them, don't let it ruin your love life: instead, get expert advice.

Help is now available through various excellent medical and counselling organizations. Please do not put yourself into the hands of one of those dodgy private clinics which advertise widely to the public – and whose main purpose is to relieve you of thousands of pounds!

If you have difficulty in finding an organization which could help you, do send me an s.a.e. at: EPS Ltd., Maddox House, 1 Maddox Street, London, W1S 2PZ. I'll try and suggest someone who could help you get your sex life back on track again.

Good luck – and good lovemaking!

INDEX

N

Narbonne position,
105–107
'Non–Doctor', 86

O

O'Connell, Helen, 54
Oscillating umbilicus
sign, 134

P

Paddles, 137–139
Penile Ridge, 42–43
Penile–Shaped vibrator,
89
Penis Enhancement rings,
98
Penisator, 92
Pjur, 8
Postillionage, 79, 126
Premature Ejaculation,
117–118
Pressure, 39
Problems with
intercourse, 142–144
Prostate massage,
130–131
'Pussy', the, 57, 59

R

Rear Entry, 42–47, 73, 87

S

Seville position, 108–109
Sex aids, 83–98, 131–139
Sex Play, 122
Simultaneous orgasm,
120–123
Spoons, 44–45
Strauss position, 104–105
Stretchy Silicone Penis
Enhancement, 98
Swift Rachel, 48

T

Thai beads, 134
Thumb on clitoris, 71
Tongue Joy, 89
Toy Boy position, 130

V

Venus Butterfly, 87–88
Vibrators, 86–92
Vibrators, rectal, 134
Vielle, the, 92–94

W

Whipple, 116

SOME MORE TITLES AVAILABLE FROM THE EPS:

SEXCITEMENT: LYNN PAULA RUSSELL

Sexcitement is a brilliant guide for couples who need to review and revitalise a tired sex life, or even just add some spice to their love-making. Combines very personal accounts guiding both male and female readers along a path of discovery – promoting pure erotic pleasure without prejudice.

£19.95

SEX PLAY: DR DAVID DELVIN

In this book dedicated solely to foreplay for advanced lovers, Dr. Delvin reveals new sex play techniques that will intensify the sensations you and your partner experience. By following his methods and Lynn Paula Russell's beautiful drawings, you will be able to excite your partner and increase your own sexual pleasure beyond ecstasy. Includes sixty additional pictures from EPS artist Monica Guevara.

£19.95

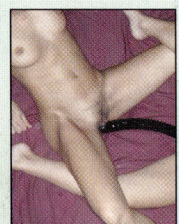

MASTERCLASS: SEX TOYS

Another first for the EPS, this book takes a critical and informative look at the veritable toy cupboard of sex toys on sale at the moment and picks the best. Then we try them out! Illustrated with stylish colour photographs this book fearlessly test-drives some of the wildest sex toys on the market. Extremely explicit!

£12.50

MASTERCLASS: BLOW JOBS

From the first tentative kiss to 'deep throat', Blow-Jobs is stuffed with information on technique, tips and ordinary people's extraordinary views on the subject. Erotically photographed and amusingly written, this little book examines every facet of the ancient art of fellatio. As important for men as it is for women!

£12.50

SEXUAL ODYSSEY: LYNN PAULA RUSSELL

Her journey of sexual self-awareness, her discovery of pleasure through pain and submission and the huge collection of her work displayed here all make Paula Russell's A Sexual Odyssey an exceptionally desirable book. Her beautifully observed and highly explicit images (many using herself as a model) mainly portray the world of corporal punishment: the female bottom is chastised in an unbelievable variety of ways.

£19.95

ORDERLINE: 0871 7110 134
EMAIL: EROS@EROTICPRINTS.ORG
SEX TOYS CAN BE FOUND ON OUR WEBSITE:
WWW.EROTICPRINTS.ORG
PLEASE CONTACT US FOR A FREE CATALOGUE